NOT JUST
ANOTHER JOB

TOM JACKSON

TIMES ⒯ BOOKS

RANDOM HOUSE

NOT JUST ANOTHER JOB

*How to Invent a Career That Works
for You—Now and in the Future*

Portions of this work were originally published in different form in *The Hidden
Job Market* by Tom Jackson and Davidyne Mayleas (Quadrangle/Times Books:
Copyright © 1976 by Tom Jackson and Davidyne Mayleas) and *The Hidden Job
Market For the 80's* by Tom Jackson and Davidyne Mayleas (Quadrangle/Times
Books: Copyright © 1976, 1981 by Tom Jackson and Davidyne Mayleas).

Library of Congress Cataloging-in-Publication Data

Jackson, Tom.
Not just another job : how to invent a career that works for you—
now and in the future / Tom Jackson.—
1st ed.
p.   cm.
ISBN 0–8129–1845–2
1. Vocational guidance.   2. Career development.   3. Career
changes.   4. Job Hunting.   I. Title.
HF5381.J365   1992
650.14—dc20   91-50189

Manufactured in the United States of America

9 8 7 6 5 4 3 2 1

First Edition

This book derives from the fundamental proposition that the fullest expression of one's personal freedom is the chosen relationship to a productive, satisfying working life. It is written at a time of global upheaval, a time when many nations—Eastern bloc and so-called Third World—are emerging from the tyranny of markets without goods and work without choice.

I dedicate this book to the workers of the emerging economies, with the hope that soon their lives will offer the career freedoms that we in the West enjoy and the possibility for creative self-expression in work that is mankind's true birthright.

ACKNOWLEDGMENTS

More than a basketful of thank-you notes is due to the many people who helped shape the ideas and the production of *Not Just Another Job*. Included in the list is, of course, Davidyne Mayleas, whose creative confidence helped in the first book, *The Hidden Job Market*. Jerry Lee gave his best work ever in typing and retyping the more than 100,000 words that were finally shaped by the sharp clean pencils and Post-it flags of the top-quality Times Books editors, led by Ruth Fecych and Trent Duffy. Barney Collier helped more than he knows, and Alexandra French was a whiz in helping shape the final layout.

Thank you all.

THE PURPOSE
OF THIS BOOK

Your career is a voyage and you are at the helm.

And the seas you are traveling are not calm. We are in turbulent times—employment is unpredictable, shrinking, and changing in many ways that have impacted, and will continue to impact, us significantly. The world economy is in shock, the environment is gravely ill, and the world political order is unpredictable and dangerous.

This book will help you estimate the risks, patch the leaks, weather the storms, choose the destinations, and avoid the rocks and shoals that block the course of a successful career. The turbulent climate of the 1990s and beyond holds new perils and challenges. By sharp planning and strategic action you can not only survive the perils, but use the forces of change to attain new heights of personal success.

The stakes are high: With the massive levels of change in virtually every field and enterprise, your very freedom of movement, livelihood, and personal fulfillment depend on exercising imagination, daring, courage, and the highest quality thinking. In this book we provide maps, charts, rules of the road, and forecasts you will find useful in achieving a high quality working life and career.

There are two parts to this book. Part One, "Career Maps," presents five essays about social, economic, technical, entrepreneurial, philosophical, and psychological domains of change you will need to take into consideration. Our information is based upon the expertise, best estimates, good guesses, and fine intuition of many seasoned explorers and observers of work, jobs, and careers. Still, as Charles Handy, a leading international management consultant and author of *The Age of Unreason,* asserts, our present state of unpredictable change is occurring at a rate that puts security about our future careers at risk.

Part Two, "The Career Voyage," is a complete course in finding the right job for you. Not just another job, but a job that meets your own personal and unique set of wishes, qualities, and interests, and matches your skills creatively with the opportunities a complex marketplace offers. A selection of information, ideas, and tactics are presented that you can use to make the practical job search into new career waters smarter, safer, more fun, and more profitable.

Not Just Another Job is for people who are thoughtful enough to prepare themselves completely and fearlessly plan ahead to get what they want. Part One will *forewarn* you of many unbridled forces, new game rules, potential pitfalls, and public and private undercurrents that must be evaded or mastered. These essays illuminate the visible and invisible principles and concepts that could become the main drivers of the global jobscape in this decade and beyond.

By examining the job-market topography, you will be best able to plan routes around problems and toward happier and more rewarding possibilities. Part Two contains powerful job-search strategies developed by specialists over the past thirty years. They will *forearm* you.

A successful voyage and a masterly career search are equal challenges. They require thorough preparation and bravery. *Not Just Another Job* is your guide and sourcebook for the journey.

BEFORE YOU CAST OFF

We believe that, regardless of your age, circumstances, or position, you are responsible for the way your work life works out. There are risks associated with this responsibility: failure, hard work, loneliness, lack of certainty, and no one to pass the buck to. And there are rewards: adventure, integration of family and occupation, control of your time, and ongoing personal growth. It is to these aims that this book is committed.

CONTENTS

The Purpose of This Book

Part One

—————————□—————————

CAREER MAPS

Changes in the world around us greatly impact our career futures. It is vital therefore that we take these external circumstances seriously into account as we plot our strategies. Part One of this book explores many issues that we believe to be essential to your understanding of how to plot the best direction for your career.

For decades the United States exported its home-grown inventions and ideals to the world at large. Its product-based industries, technology, consumer society, expanded educational base, and service sector, as well as the quest for a constantly improving standard of living, fueled both commercial and personal growth. Those ideas took root abroad, nurtured by the primacy and persuasion of global media, the sheer physical dominance of the American Way, and the growth of a multinational culture fueled initially by American enterprise.

In the recent past, American progress has seriously slowed and even declined. Resources we once considered unlimited have become scarce, eaten up by national debt, business failures, and waste. In addition, the decay of the physical and social infrastructure has handicapped our future. Career mobility has been dampened just as it was rising.

And yet, within this environment of decline, an upturn can be seen. It is possible to observe the reemergence of American inventiveness. It is showing up in some of the new ways people are considering their work and jobs. Unlike almost any other people, Americans are more than ever espousing a free market in jobs. Our willingness to manage our own careers rather than let them be "system managed" stands out in the world. The idea that one can shop around for the best offer, look to change careers midstream, or be a full-time free-lancer is radical thinking in most countries and is just starting to take hold in Western Europe. Through this kind of personal initiative, career voyagers like you will prosper, even in the roughest times. Ultimately, the economy as a whole will benefit.

Here are some examples of new American career trends:

□ According to Chicago outplacement consultants Challenger, Gray and Christmas, Inc., more Americans than ever are building their own small businesses, upgrading or changing their list of skills, and going back to school.

□ The American Association of Retired Persons claims that more people over fifty are leaving their old jobs in the monoliths and entering the work force in new ways. The old idea of simply retiring to the back porch or the golf links has been replaced by the concept of part-time work and stints as "interim managers" (medium-term management contracts for free-lance execs).

□ The worldwide competition for business and among businesses means higher requirements for quality, innovation, and global understanding. American job-seekers are getting the message and learning how to develop cross-cultural thinking.

□ With the rapid expansion of personal computers and information networks and an American fluidity in work styles, we are strongly positioned for the Information Age, where transactions are no longer face-to-face but terminal to terminal and network to network. The locus for getting the job done has moved beyond the formal office to the home, car, ski lodge, or community. Home base is becoming the data base.

Because of the depth of change in this country and abroad, today's career voyager must be prepared with the latest navigational information. If you try to work this new terrain with old maps, you are going to run aground. This book recharts the career currents and brings the maps and rules of the road up to date.

Career Map 1:

---□---

UNCERTAINTY

A singular lesson taught by twentieth-century business practices is that long-lasting job security is no longer to be expected or perhaps even desired. There is no predictable set of behaviors or career choices that will guarantee job security. Uncertainty and unpredictability are all that *is* certain. It is imperative to learn to accept and defuse the fear and disorientation that usually accompany uncertainty in an arena as important as one's career. While it is normal to be anxious at times, this fear, if allowed to go too far, can shut down one's thinking. Fortunately, opportunities are another by-product of upheaval, and they are almost always greater than the dangers in a dynamic economy. By being able to shift to a more creative response, one can prosper while others are frozen with inaction. Challenges and opportunities are two sides of the same coin. What frightens one person motivates another.

Consider these challenges:

- □ You read one day that a competitor has introduced a new piece of technology as good as yours for half the price. Your options: to get out of the business and change jobs, or to interpret the competitor's breakthrough as an opportunity to use this new technology to make your products better.
- □ Your factories have been given six months to clear up thirty years of pollution and environmental abuse. You are the PR director.

□ You meet your new boss for the first time and discover that "he" is an Asian woman five years younger than you are. Your expectations are blasted.

□ Your spouse comes home with a promotion that requires a relocation to a place you don't want to go.

□ Your boss sits you down to a cup of coffee and tells you the department is being eliminated.

If these particular uncertainty scenarios aren't relevant to your own career, dozens of others are. Anticipating the unexpected is a useful protection against surprise upsets. For example, getting advance warning about bad news in your own industry, even though the impact to your own organization may be two years away, will give you the time to store resources, upgrade capabilities, or get your network humming.

Then there is the totally unexpected event. You may start by being confident that you are slicker and quicker and that you possess more personal reserves and a stronger mind than almost anyone you know. And yet uncertainty will still sneak up and surprise you. You watch last year's industry leader get busted on the stock market and a tremor lands in your gut. When dealing with the unanticipated, resist the tendency to respond with old tools and approaches. Instead, let the event cool off and then interpret what's going on in ways that could empower you. When an unexpected event shows up, pull back, breathe deeply, walk around the block—depersonalize it.

❖ **Rule of the road:** *Convert problems to opportunities.*

When we react fearfully to something that jeopardizes us, we usually "worry" the problem—engage in endless inner conversations that play to our least powerful sides. The mind sees the worst, the stress points clamp down, the jaw sets, and our thinking goes on autopilot or shuts down entirely.

For many, the inbred tendency is to react to the fear of unemployment and take a survivalist approach, grabbing the first piece of career flotsam that comes along and clinging to its limited advantages for the rest of one's career. We look at economic disturbances and say, Things are getting bad; let's cut back. We fulfill our own negative prophecies. Most often the nay-sayers say it louder than the yea-sayers.

Instead of focusing on the difficulties and hazards, raise this question: What new situations does this present that I didn't see before? You can discover new work opportunities that will enrich your relationship with your family, help you reduce stress, give you the chance to learn new skills, and make your working life better fit your current view of yourself.

Multiply the Possibilities

Uncertainty is studded with infinite possibilities, whereas certainty is a small, single thing. In the future, we must come to understand that there are few long-term career commitments. By shifting the thinking from thoughts of scarcity (Help! The unemployment rate is 9 percent.) to a context of abundance (The *employment* rate is 91 percent—good odds, better than ten to one in my favor.), the mind's ability to create is multiplied.

Move from "But" to "And"

For every reason to move forward, you can find a rational reason to hold back: I want to start a small business, *but* there isn't enough money; I want to learn the computer, *but* I don't have time; I want to work in Europe, *but* I speak only English. The internal litany goes on: it's crazy, or nobody's ever done it before, or it hurts, or I can't get up that early, and on and on.

You can move beyond the constraints of this either/or system of thinking, from *but* (which implies mutual exclusivity in both the language and our thinking) to *and*. The mind-set that says, I want to work close to home, *but* I don't know of any job openings shifts to I want to work close to home, *and* I don't know of any openings *yet*. Our ability to create positive change is directly linked to the way we think, and this thinking is often constrained by old language.

Think about this: A job is an opportunity to solve a problem. There can be no scarcity of jobs, since there is a seemingly limitless supply of problems. Unfortunately there *is* a scarcity of people daring enough to recognize or operate from the point of view of solutions. Different cultures and organizations are stuck in widely differing views of the world, often based on deeply rooted traditions and values. It is productive, and also profitable, to bring a fresh viewpoint to an old culture.

Asking powerful questions can help you break away from old constraints and uncertainties to new ways of seeing things. How do I want it to be? is far more powerful than What's going to happen to me now? Look for ways to pose questions that empower your thinking.

Know Who You Really Are

You are not your job title. You are not your degree. You are not who your spouse or parents think you are, or what society defines. In a world of uncertainty, labels or characterizations anchor us to the past. Old thinking based on old labels or imprisoned by old ways of speaking limits how you express yourself. It puts boundaries on your talent. It tends to make you smaller than you are.

Take a fresh inventory of your strengths that goes beyond your last job description. In Part Two, we provide you with a guide to making this reassessment.

Keep a Vision in View

The quest for certainty keeps our view of the world in the grips of the familiar. If we learn to view uncertainty as an ally, we can create a new picture of the way things are or could be. Through an enlarged vision, we can free ourselves from the chains of our history. A vision answers the question, If things were as I really wanted them to be, what would they look like? Virtually all creative movement comes from vision. If I wish an ideal vacation, I create it in my mind first. If I want to win at power tennis, I visualize where I want the balls to go and get them there.

Clear vision ignites the will. All too frequently the potential for vision deteriorates into tired pictures of disillusionment, failure, sadness, and fear of the consequences. We stop short of taking creative action to protect ourselves from the anxiety of an uncertain future.

Our ability to see and interpret events creatively often disintegrates into mediocrity when we act to protect ourselves from the anxiety of uncertainty.

Today's successful career entrepreneurs are masters of vision who continually invent and build new possibilities out of uncertainty. They have no problem merging dreams they are passionate about with methods that are practical. They are the progenitors of new landscapes, new systems, and new ways of living and working. They are unwilling to settle for just another job.

Career Map 2:

—◻—

STRANGENESS

Ours is a world in which the idea of lifetime employment, the comfortable certainty of a predictable future, has been undermined by the complexities of external change. Not only are the times uncertain, but there is also a disturbing quality of strangeness in what we confront in day-to-day work and in the career quest. There are new values, locations, cultures, currencies, languages, working rules, power bases, manners, and technologies to contend with.

Most Americans believe that our culture has enough resiliency to pull us through periods of adversity. We can hear American pop music in a tavern in Torremolinos or Rome or Moscow, find brand-name business concepts in play in multinationals, and recognize the influences we have had (and still have) in mass culture. So it is easy to be misled. Unfortunately, we must acknowledge that, although we have a history of being technically superior and commercially adept, the years of de facto American business leadership are long gone. Much of what you confront as a global career voyager will be strange and no longer secure.

The best multinational organization is a multicultural organism.

By extending your perspective a few years, you can see the emergence and prevalence of a new world order of work. Multinational companies are being transformed into organizations that truly integrate diverse nationalities and cultures into day-to-day transactions—getting the best *from* all *for* all. For example:

□ A company with an American computer makes transactions in German to a Saudi Arabian bank, for the purpose of selling property in Brazil to pay for movie rights in Hollywood.

□ The treasurer of Citibank Italia spends more time talking to the treasurer in New York City than he does to his own peers in Naples.

□ An American cosmetics firm that buys fragrances in France in order to develop a new line of Argentine cosmetics is taking risks that include the political and trade issues of the countries concerned. Beyond business as usual by two continents.

□ A technocrat in Austria may speak more comfortably with a technocrat in Ottawa than with his own cousin in Zurich.

A new career system is arising, one that is not mainly national or ethnic. This multicultural interplay will be uncomfortable and strange at first. By keeping yourself flexible, setting aside old biases, and adapting quickly, you will be able to overcome the disorientation that can accompany such quick changes of scene and scenario. Your career voyage will be global in scope.

The knitting together of cultures is beyond tribalism. The fabric of cross-cultural economic interests militates against the kind of nationalistic wars we've had in the past. The interconnected globalism in business and consumerism is eclipsing the political systems in power. The failure of the Eastern bloc's Communist governments is more a failure of economics than political rhetoric. In Moscow, McDonald's arches are more popular than the Museum of the Revolution.

Managing your career at the global level requires new competencies. Where there are risks, there are rewards. World-class career voyagers with strong aspirations have an opportunity to create new models of career entrepreneurism. To work successfully in cultures beyond the United States, you must operate with new principles. These include:

□ *Respect* for people and styles you don't yet understand. Listen deeply before judging what's right or wrong.

□ *Flexibility* in tuning or adjusting your work style and job-seeking approaches to meet new customs that might never have occurred to you or that seem antiquated or stupid.

□ The *courage* to stop, look, and listen before acting. Avoid the self-righteousness that created the Ugly American and that still shows up in American-dominated businesses abroad.

□ The recognition that *value added* is the overriding principle in business and personal managing today. You must always consider adding to systems that work, rather than instinctively tearing them down and starting over. You must learn how to express your skills and qualities in terms of helping, rather than in terms of taking over. In a recent example, a respected American training firm lost a major opportunity to train in Europe because it insisted on delivering the American version of a successful training program and pressed too hard and too fast against the cultural reserves of the client. The Americans ran from strangeness rather than embracing it and adding value.

In a world of diversity and strangeness, there is great room for new leadership in nontraditional forms. The leader with the broadest vision will get the most followers. This new diversity invalidates nationalism and even, to an extent, patriotism. It is a new supranationalism. Career leadership has the same requirement: a broad vision by which strangeness and uncertainty are perceived as opportunities for creating new ways of working, not just another job.

Future Possibility Bulletin I. From the mid- to late 1990s on, the senior economic powers of the world will be forced to mount a combined ecological rescue effort that surpasses any previous peaceful international venture in history.

Future Possibility Bulletin II. Allegiance to national flags and boundaries is becoming conditional. Poles flock to Germany, Kurds to Iran, and Hong Kong Chinese to Singapore and Canada. Mexicans continue to migrate to North America. The USSR breaks into ethnic republics, which realign into economic trading partners. Barriers that have restrained truly significant transnational social and political movements fall as fast as trade blocks.

Future Possibility Bulletin III. Relative ease and speed of transportation and tele- and videocommunication make it possible to plan an appointment in Perth on Tuesday, a dinner in Tel Aviv on Friday, dancing in London on Saturday night, and a few days in New York beginning Sunday evening, without losing touch with the home office. Of course, you can reach almost anyone in seconds or minutes through telecommunications hookups with computer translations. In the scope of these communications, the idea of personal networks takes on much greater meaning and importance, and truer understanding will be achieved by using these networks than in traditional meetings.

COMING BACK HOME
□

The diversity of cultures in the United States has never been greater. As ever, people follow money: Japanese, Koreans, Taiwanese, and other Asians have by now so much invested in American markets that they are sending people by the thousands to help manage it and make it grow. On the darker side, untrained immigrants from the Third World and unskilled American minorities fill the lower depths of the labor pool. Strange and threatening contrasts between haves and have-nots make the job market complex. A career voyager must approach the work environment with as few racial or ethnic biases as possible. The business world is today's great melting pot.

A career voyager supervising a diverse work force must be open to new ways of interacting: including trusting intuition, empowering, coaching, helping teams manage themselves, and relying on humor and forgiveness.

CRITICAL CHOICES
□

If, individually and corporately, we continue to treat change as hostile and fall back on avoidance, denial, and protectionism, we can reasonably predict the decline of American enterprise as we have known it—and of our own personal career possibilities. Protectionism will keep us from challenging ourselves: learning new things, upgrading our vision of the future, and reaping the rewards of working to our full potential.

When we view change—even when it comes cloaked in strangeness—as opportunity, we will be able to create fresh visions, discard outmoded work-styles, and step outside of boundaries that have become routine and stale. We will reinvent and refresh our organizations and institutions and remodel our careers to meet new family and community aims. We will stay youthful in our attitude and approach. With this vitality the work we do will take on a new efficiency and our organizations will prosper.

INTERNATIONALISM

□

If you enter a conference of Italians and are put off by the loudness, cacophony, gesticulation, and impassioned self-expression, you are probably lost. In Palermo a business conference may seem to you to be a street fight; in Amsterdam it might feel like a wake. Learn to step out of old roles and step into new neighborhoods despite the strangeness. You are not a tourist in the new world order—you are a *participant*. Leave your fear in the hotel. A career voyager moves away from the comfort of familiarity and into the local marketplaces. Find someone who can translate (or, even better, learn the language yourself) and engage: communicate, communicate, communicate; listen, listen, listen.

A career internationalist will have insights into what the world's new markets are all about. There are new ways of selling, new needs to satisfy, new services to provide. None of this can be learned unless one embraces the inherent strangeness of the international scene. Thinking that your favorite cuisine or your style of dress, religion, or method of cost accounting is the only valid one is both cocky and insecure. Your conviction may be charming for a while, but it will keep you outside the gates when the real business is going down. When an American banking giant took over a large Southern Italian chain, the new owners made the Italians feel as if they did not know their profession—even though Italians have been bankers for two thousand years. The Americans' arrogance stood in the way of instituting the kind of collaborative improvements that were the reason for the merger in the first place. The cost of this blindness was in the megamillions.

People in some cultures are too polite to tell you you are making mistakes. Instead, they will unintentionally sabotage you through silence. If you are about to be beheaded, they might not even raise a whisper. A career internationalist must make the assumption—even when confronted with apparent evidence to the contrary—that people in *all* cultures are fundamentally intelligent and cooperative and that they want to feel respected and to make things work.

A danger is that in a new terrain we may choose to hire people who look and think like us, and so fail to use diversity to our advantage. If we stick to our old ways for too long, one day the tables may turn and we will be bossed by people who refuse to understand us.

Uniformity and conformity are dated concepts. To prosper in your work life, your thinking must stay open. In order to be effective, you must challenge old assumptions and invent new ways to get problems solved.

Successful career voyagers train themselves to recognize *similarities*. They base understandings and actions upon points of mutual contact. Such skill in spotting similarities is sharpened by almost daily practice. As an American manager in a new culture, it is essential to ask a lot of questions, get things clear, hire good advisors, and find a pilot who knows the local waters.

❖ **Rule of the road:** *Communicate action and possibility.*

When on foreign turf, start by noticing the surroundings, the body language, and the centers of influence—who defers to whom, which people collect others around them. Monitor your own body language. Be relaxed but avoid posturing. Be observant. Watch how the locals behave. Go slow. Show respect and courtesy. Ask sincere questions that can elicit people's feelings about the scope of any planned activities and their hopes and visions for the occasion before elaborating your own ideas. Listen to the background sounds and be sensitive to the emotional tone.

Language and communication savvy are among the most important tools of the trade for the career voyager.

Future Possibility Bulletin IV.   An English-only resume relegates twenty-first century managers to well-defined boundaries and vastly limits their mobility. The most successful careerists are multilingual. It is not uncommon for the leader of a nation as powerful as the United States to speak several tongues fluently, be entirely computer literate, play a sport well, and speak to crowds of people in a way that gets them to listen and even to laugh in good humor.

Future Possibility Bulletin V.   Linguistic-software development laboratories are scattered about the globe. You can now brush up on French or Arabic with laser-disk computer packages that teach languages with interactive video and exciting computer games that teach the right things to say in the new language.

When you see strangeness as an invitation to explore your future courageously, you will trade in what you fear for what supports you in getting the right career.

Career Map 3:

BREAKING
OUT OF BOXES

A major problem in launching an innovative career search arises from a fundamental misunderstanding of one's true starting point and potential. We are so used to relying on appearances that the underlying truths of our situations often remain masked. The degree, job title, past experience, and visible strengths and weaknesses take front billing as what we have to offer. Advertised jobs, work we are familiar with, self-taught limitations, obsolete career requirements, and a narrow view of the employment market (the unemployment rate is 10 percent—there are no jobs out there) . . . constrain our view of what we can "legitimately" hope for.

Being unaware of your true embarkation point often means you don't notice when your thinking is faulty or incomplete. While your career aspirations may seem clear, progress can be blindsided by frozen attitudes, opinions, and beliefs that have long gone unchallenged. Most of us have lived so long with a fixed set of ideas about our work, careers, and potential that new ideas or approaches are virtually unthinkable.

EXPLODING THE LIMITS OF ORDINARY THOUGHT

For our purposes, a box is any interpretation of reality that constrains growth. It's an invisible structure (or paradigm) within which we operate, one that allows for no surprises or adventures. We accept the way things are.

Breaking out of boxes is a process of discovering and tearing down those walls that restrict our ability to see and know the full realm of possibility. It is about creating new realities that can open greater space for the union of work and life.

Knowing how to break out of boxes is a must for anyone who needs an innovative solution to an old problem or a fresh, new opportunity in a tired situation. Breaking out of boxes is an essential skill for building the kind of career triumphs that you seek. It is a key ingredient in the larger tasks of building your future—individually, in your family, and within work organizations.

For example, it can be life-saving to discover that taking the wrong job can be more costly than the salary in terms of stress, poor self-esteem, and limited personal development. It is especially important to realize that we can design our own work situations, to realize in middle age that up is not the only way to go. One can move *out* to new levels of participation, involvement, self-expression, and joy. To create a new game, we often need to close a familiar old game board and throw away the pieces.

A fundamental method for discovering the borders of your thinking about your career is to pose challenging new questions:

Instead of asking: How does someone my age [fifty] find a new job?
Ask: Which of today's vexing problems do I want to work on?

Instead of asking: Are there any openings for me?
Ask: What am I best at?

Instead of asking: How can I possibly live on less?
Ask: How do I put more quality moments into my life?

And, the most powerful career planning questions: How do I want my life to be? And what will that look like?

We construct or invent the meaning of our boxes ourselves, and then hide the fact that we made it all up. The constructed reality gets its force through the interpretations we give it. To us there are so-called good jobs and so-called bad jobs, and we all seem to *know* which are which. The good people get the good jobs and live happily ever after, and the bad people plod along. We should admit it . . . we do think that way. We are comfortable in one job reality, then one day the fashion changes, the once fast-track organizations have turned into draconian polluters, and *green* jobs are hot tickets.

The interpretations that guide or control our thinking could be called thinking habits. They come, like the family jewels, from older regimes. They are the product of our parents' social classes, our own early experiences of breaking away and starting fresh, societal values that we pick up unconsciously, and the power and convictions of past successes. These old thinking habits tell us: If it worked once, it ought to work again.

These habits and values have gained strong support because we tend to associate with those people who agree with us, to read those papers that we agree with, and to bad-mouth that which is new and slightly brazen. We assert the old reality and then try to keep it in place. The good old folks get promoted for the wrong reasons and then need to be committed to the systems that got them there. Decaying and decadent bureaucracies hold on tight.

Careers themselves take on the quality of connected boxes. We study hard and get a fancy degree. We invest time and energy into building a trajectory. We feel good and we try new things. While some ideas succeed, others go unappreciated and we stop doing them. Some time later we wake up, look out the window, and notice that we're gazing at an old landscape. The career plateau sets in, and we are told that this is the nature of the middle years. Don't believe it.

A box is rigid and apparently secure. The threatening changes are taking place outside the box. As Michael de St. Arnaud, author of *NewSell*, observed, the truth is that any box is simply the *current view of the situation* (the CVS). By approaching that reality as only a current view of the situation, we open the possibility that there is a *better view of the situation* (the BVS), from which many alternative interpretations and directions are possible. Since there are many possible interpretations or meanings to most situations, the rule for a self-correcting and improving reality is to choose the interpretation that empowers your life to be the way you want it to be. The little voice inside your head (the CVS) says, Don't bother trying—they'll never hire you because you don't have the education the ad said they required. The view from outside the box (the BVS) says, I bet they'll see me if I can prove that my practical experience is better than a degree. It works, and with practice the old reality breaks away like a fortune cookie.

The walls of a box are the interpretations, beliefs, opinions, and assumptions we have collected. Once in place they remain hidden for most of us until outside dynamics cast the box against the rocks and a breakdown occurs. The career master knows how to dissolve the boxes along the way, avoiding unexpected breakdowns and inventing new ways of working and thinking. When you get stuck in one interpretation—for example, They won't hire me because I'm too old—ask the power question, *How do I know that?* The BVS will tell you: Perhaps I don't present myself in the best way; I'll do a better resume.

INVENTING A FRAMEWORK THAT FITS YOUR NEEDS
□

There are many ways to get your mind to recognize new interpretations and new points of view on old situations. The point is not to come up with the "right" or "wrong" way of looking at things, but to discover how many *different* interpretations you can develop. In doing this, you release natural creativity and tap into greater resources that allow new opportunities to emerge.

One way to approach this is through brainstorming. Brainstorming is, of course, the process of finding as many answers to a powerful and relevant question as possible without judging whether they are "good" or "bad." It's an excellent way to discover multiple solutions or perspectives to a problem or situation. For example, if you have finally had it with commuting two hours every day and have not found a solution, you could begin by asking yourself, How much of my job could be done from a home in the country? or What new skills do I need to be marketable despite location? If you still can't come up with anything, you haven't yet broken out of the box. Invite some of your most creative friends to contribute, play at it, list new things that your smaller self thinks are unrealistic. Make a long and inventive list.

Another way to dissolve the constraints of career boxes is to interact with others outside your particular field or role. If you work in production, socialize with people in advertising or marketing. If you have most of your experience in education, network with computer folks. Because our boxed-in patterns are so interconnected with people, and the places and old ideas associated with those people, we have to step outside these familiar relationships, even if the payoff isn't obvious—*particularly* if the payoff isn't obvious.

Freeing yourself from confining patterns opens a fertile array of new pathways to follow and new options to consider as you move toward your goal. Outside the box, you discover that personal progress isn't a function of making the right contacts, choosing the right companies, and doing the right thing every step of the way, all based on old mental models. You'll find that any number of paths can lead you to where you wish to go if you are open to the myriad possibilities that lie just over the horizon. Imagination combined with courage equals a new future that you design. Not just another job.

THE SIREN SONG OF SUCCESS

Among the most seductive pitfalls you are likely to face during your career are the very goodies that strengthen the hold of a familiar job box.

The gnawing frustration caused by doing work that we really don't want to do is obscured by rewards that keep us riding the rails of imagined success. This cycle is easy to follow: We take a job that doesn't truly turn us on because we need the money; and we talk ourselves into this betrayal of our dreams with the excuse that it is only for a few months, until something better comes along. Until we get our act together. Days pass into weeks, weeks into months, to seasons, to a few years, and . . . we forget. The job gets easier, we are recognized for our skills, the small raises come with the bills. Our friends are from work.

And then one day, out of the corners of our eyes, we catch a glimpse of a career outrider wearing our dream colors and our hearts sink. We get out the old folder and try to build a fresh resume, but the words are just not there for us. We think in terms of our current job, and the best we can think to say about ourselves seems right off yesterday's job posting. We ask, and are told that the dream jobs are all tied up right now—please call back. Our heart hurts for a few weeks, and then a big task lands on our desk and we are pressed into service. The ego tells the heart to wait.

A few more years go by, and—suddenly—we have a *career,* marked by a title, credentials, influence in the company, an identity built on what we've done. More friends. By now, we might occasionally talk about our dreams in the past tense ("When I was younger . . ."). More time passes. A rude awakening: This is your niche. You've made it to the top. This is as far as you can go on this ladder. A plateau comes into view. Your ship has docked.

BREAKING OUT: INVENTING A NEW REALITY

You wake up to the question of whether working in a job you are only mildly interested in, for a firm that you don't really like very much, is a net benefit or a net cost. In searching for the answer, you reassess the relationship of your work to your life and realize that they are interconnected. You are living out most of your time at the company. Yikes! This *is* my life. With courage and support you call the job what it is—an imitation of your true self at work. You cast off the lines, hoist the sails, and set out against the tide, bound for new adventures.

Within the game of career, whole environments conspire in the illusion that the playing field and reality are one; they win our allegiance to "the way things are." Breaking out of this takes more than openness or imagination—it takes a genuine act of courage, a commitment to your bigger self and the quality of your future life.

The courage to question the unquestionable is the beginning of a breakthrough. Now you must bring your creativity to bear on finding answers to your questions. This is the time to make new inventories and to risk what you are for what you might become. To give up what's merely good for what could be great.

How does such a game get created? How does a box get built? In view of our human attachment to security, how can we ever muster the strength to turn our backs on the past? The first step is to challenge some fundamental old ideas we have been taught all our lives.

Old View: Work — New View: Life

In the old view, work is how you make a living from nine to five, five days a week, for forty or more years. Life itself—the real you, the one who pays the final tab—seems reserved for after five and on weekends, a few weeks off each year and then . . . retirement . . . the big vacation. Most of us have invested so much in a work/life polarity that it is hard to think of another view. "I've got a good-paying job, I spend some time with the kids, the weekends come and go, the rent gets paid, who said work is supposed to be fun," says the steelworker at a Rust Belt bar and grill. Indeed, who said? The universality of such things as happy hours, elation at quitting time, and expressions like "Thank God it's Friday" attests to the strength and pervasiveness of one of the largest boxes our culture has invented: Work is where you earn the right to have your life.

In a truer view, work and life are the words and music to the same ballad. We are living while at work. We are alive—even if it doesn't often look that way. Since we spend about 10,000 priceless days on the job, many of the people we come to know are at the office or plant, and work is where we make our mark and secure our wealth, it behooves us to make sure we're getting the biggest bounce from every minute we invest and that the work we do reflects a life worth living. The challenge for career voyagers is to venture into areas that challenge, satisfy, enliven, and inspire—and that help form a whole fabric in which family, community, social, and personal values combine to enrich and nurture one another each working day.

Old View: Need — New View: Value

From our earliest days we're informed directly and through the cultural icons that everyone "needs" a job. Dads and moms come home tired, complaining about the pressure to pay for our food and shelter. So-called good jobs seem to buy dignity and esteem and to be a passport to public stature, and a foundation for our identity among our peers. The need to get the right job keeps the schools grinding. Little wonder that searching for another job from this perspective becomes grim and serious business. We go on interviews and write resumes with all the joy of a visit to the dentist.

Outside this box we can discover the view that a job does not merely fill an external need; it is also an offer for an exchange of values (as well as time) for money. By shifting our orientation from one of balancing job and money needs to one of combining personal values with the work we do, we open a new conversation: How can I help get the job done in a way that enriches both the company's goals and objectives and my own? is a bigger question than Do you have any openings? When you see your work as a vehicle for serving the needs of a person or organization whose values you admire and respect, you present yourself not as a problem, but as a problem-solver. You are a creator of assets rather than an expense.

❖ **Rule of the road**: *Any employer will hire any individual if the employer is convinced that it will bring more value than it costs.*

The key to satisfying employment, reemployment, and redeployment is our creative ability to solve problems, to make opportunities, and to act from the values that we bring. Seeing this, our conversation shifts from What's in it for me? to What can I contribute, what solutions can I provide?

Old View: Scarcity — New View: Abundance

The longest-running career commentary—through good times and bad, from new grads to old hands—is: There are no [none of the right kind of] jobs out there. The conventional wisdom that good jobs are hard to find is a major box. The law of supply and demand seems to dictate that worthwhile, valuable jobs are scarce. (What we really see as scarce are the slots in someone's hiring chart or line items on a budget.)

By casting yourself as a solution finder rather than a job-seeker, your conversation takes you from the realm of need to the realm of value. In so doing, you state not what you want from an employer but the benefit and value you bring. As a problem solver you can see an abundance of opportunity.

Old View: Standard of Living — New View: Quality of Life

The chase for the standard of living is rarely finished, and there is no denying its power. From the Baltics to Baltimore, a banner reads: High(er) standard of living—*now*!

Since salaries determine one's standard of living, making more money has become the daily goal for most of humanity. However, the cost equations for this effort have gotten out of hand. Both Mom and Dad are at their desks five or six days a week to bring home the money to pay for last month's necessities. New kids on the job are keeping their phones or lasers lit up sixty hours a week to make it to bonus country.

The quality of life can't be saved up. Quality moments come from the satisfaction that what we are doing is useful and generated from inner values. It is the work itself, not the paycheck, that quickens the pulse when we have integrated living and working. It's not the job we've got that makes the difference—it's how we relate to it that counts.

In Part Two, you will find several exercises that help you put your qualities and values to work for you.

Old View: Security — New View: Versatility

Job security is a trap. Of course, we want a stable and predictable platform from which to build, a guaranteed income to plan our lives, a familiar role to play in our community and our organization. However, many millions of workers pay a very high price for these securities: hard, menial tasks for minimum wages and maximum toxicity, little autonomy, ass-kissing to stay put, immobility, few creative outlets, conformity to company work rules and political cultures. Today, even in executive suites, job security has become voluntary servitude, limiting even the most personal choices: what sports to play, what vacations to take, what marriage partners to seek. Clearly job security has done little to nourish the soul and enhance the pleasure of self-expression.

Worse, the security net often fails, and when it does, it goes in a big way. Depression-era images of men selling pencils are replaced with images of well-dressed managers lining up for the outplacement counselor and the severance check. The 1980s saw the rise and fall of the secure professional—teachers, bankers, and managers of all sorts found their claims on seniority and longevity to be worthless. For many, the comedown has been hard—no income, few savings, low self-esteem, and seemingly nowhere to go.

Yet the greatest asset human beings have is their creative ability to adapt to change. This is the only true security: the power to act in the face of risk, to create, redirect, refocus, and transform our energies as required by the vicissitudes of life. Human beings are adventuresome and resourceful. We fly, we dive; we build cathedrals and split atoms; we create art, music, and drama; we design computers and Big Macs.

Especially in this era of rapid and extensive change, versatility and courage are box-breaking qualities. We have embarked on a voyage from an old world to a new one. The invitation is there, the landmarks are charted, and others have cleared the way. What's required is a strong commitment to oneself, trust in one's own natural resourcefulness, a willingness to think strategically and to question old realities rigorously, and, above all, the courage to follow the heart.

Career Map 4:

TEC-KNOWLEDGE

The career voyager will hit turbulent seas, and one's course will need to be readjusted more than once to cope with the unfamiliar, the opportune, or the perilous. To do so, a grasp of technology and its increasing impact on our lives and careers is a critical skill for today's career professional.

Our present period of accelerating change differs in substance from the levels of change that humankind has become comfortable with. We now live in a time when change is discontinuous or unpredictable. Buckminster Fuller and Charles Handy have emphasized that technology has accelerated at such a rate that it has virtually escaped the realm of predictability.

For example, a new way to put natural gas to work efficiently could rewrite the world's energy maps. What would that mean for travel, housing, costs of manufacturing, etc.? Robotics is already a potential liberator of the physical laborer. Combine the two—inexhaustible energy and robots—and what happens to the day-to-day equations of our work lives?

❖ **Rule of the road:** *Use powerful tools.*

The average professional person has at her disposal vast technology that only a few years ago was reserved for the largest organizations:

☐ Electronic communication offers cheap and instant access to business around the world. A manufacturer in Bangkok can contact a client in

Bangor, Maine, faster than either can walk to the corner grocery store. Signed contracts are moved from Paris to Honolulu in less time than it takes to type them.

☐ In home offices throughout the world, productivity accelerates and information expands as research, strategic planning, and personal communications are facilitated by microchips, fiber optics, lasers, and other technologies incomprehensible to most of us who use them.

☐ Vast information networks can locate obscure facts and organize them specifically to our needs. Through our modems, we have access to world news and the names and locations of expanding organizations.

A savvy career voyager knows how to work with the tools of technology. Although many people will put up a valiant effort to avoid the showdown, in a decade or less the technologically illiterate will be straining to catch up. Today's middle managers are just starting to see this. A major pharmaceuticals company recently discovered that the junior employees were able to harness the company's mainframes for information and decision making directly from home or hotel, while many older executives were still having their secretaries download their computer mail. As a result, a defensive crash course was initiated to bring the technophobes back into the game.

While we may recognize the impact of technology in a broad or general way, few of us fully appreciate the extent of the personal opportunities it provides us in every aspect of our work and life. Fewer still capitalize on the enormous intellectual, professional, social, and financial advantages that computer and other technical literacy provides. The successful traveler to a powerful career future will know otherwise: The uses of technology will provide a major trading advantage.

❖ **Rule of the road:** *Do more with less.*

One of the major advantages of knowing your way around the technosphere is the leverage it provides you to get more done with less. This makes you more productive and more valuable. A key factor in building personal performance is using the power of good tools to multiply your advantage. (Imagine building a house today without a power screwdriver.) At some stage in the early acquisition of technology or new tools there is a cost peak in the learning curve, when it takes more time to do things the new way than to continue in the old. This is the trap into which most short-term systems fall: How can I take the time to learn how to type or use a keyboard when

I've got a dozen other priorities? What's missing is a commitment to investing in new ways of working. This is the hallmark of organizations and people that know how to master new challenges and prosper.

THE LEARNING ADVANTAGE OF TECHNOLOGY

□

For those who grew up before the advent of video and computer games, our children's technical fluency seems awesome. Parents today are eager to invest in the latest educational software and in the most challenging video puzzles and gadgetry that allow their kids to experiment with everything from filmmaking to financial forecasting to musical composition. In a growing number of school systems worldwide, individually paced interactive software is reversing learning deficits. Adult or child, it takes courage to sit down at a keyboard and video screen and embark on new learning. Yet this is the most fruitful avenue for the development of our fullest potential and net worth. Simulations, interactive learning games, reference libraries by phone line, and networks of special interest groups all add enormous dimension to the flow of knowledge, skill, and information. Don't overlook this incredible resource. Stay in touch and stay on top.

It is important to bring into view another arena of "technology" that is perhaps the most exciting of all: the ability to *think* in new ways. Someone once described the human mind as "a billion-bit random access computer with no software." The ability to think critically or creatively has become a victim of the widespread homogenized learning and workplace systems of past decades.

Thinking about thinking has entered a new phase. Corporations are investing in programs that map the routes to innovation and creativity in the never-ending search for more productive ways of working. Edward de Bono, the British pioneer in thought processes; Synectics, the Massachusetts-based consulting firm focused on teaching thinking skills; Roger Van Oech, author of the popular *A Wack on the Side of the Head;* and others are all in demand as we discover that new challenges cannot be met by playing the old tapes on better equipment.

Marketing, finance, human resources, manufacturing, transportation, and other high-knowledge sectors are all undergoing massive changes in the ways they get the work done. New processes, equipment, and principles need to be explored, learned, and practiced. Jobs are not static, they redefine themselves each day. A successful career voyager stays on top by reading the most advanced trade journals, attending conferences, and going out of the way to meet leaders in the field.

❖ **Rule of the road:** *Explore domains of change.*

The range of technological advances stretches beyond the horizon. No person can keep up to date on all or even a large part of it. However, we must expand our vision as far as we can and escape the boxed-in thinking that keeps us stranded on only two or three areas of interest in our lives: politics, market research, community, home/family, etc. Although it sounds mechanical, it would be useful for you to map out four or five areas beyond your normal interests, areas that—even though they may have no obvious linkage to your day-to-day life—could eventually lead you to substantial rewards.

Here are some of the domains to monitor right now. From these you can also think of derivations or new ones. Most of them are interconnected.

The Domain of Information
- [ ] Live, round-the-clock news service.
- [ ] The ability to manage personal financial resources in a multitude of ways from the home, office phone or workstation: transfer funds, invest, change insurance policies, etc. A mobile, ongoing conversation with our money.
- [ ] Market information, analysis, and media connections that can enable us to pinpoint potential users of our products simply by manipulating past predictors and income vectors and factoring in new elements. On-line simulations of strategies for market penetration.
- [ ] The ability to know what's happening in everyone else's backyard. We are able to obtain immediate, current data on birthrates, death rates, incomes, imports/exports; rain forest reversal, weather forecasts; pollution indexes; the status of various species, etc.

The Domain of Energy
- [ ] Operating safely within an energy glut and without a glut of pollution.
- [ ] Opening up avenues of solar power and alternative energy sources.
- [ ] Worldwide concern, consciousness, and partnership on energy storage and conservation.
- [ ] Developing automated, energy-conscious home and family life-styles.
- [ ] Portable power packs that keep us connected to energy without wires.

The Domain of Materials and Chemicals
□ A whole new world of biodegradable synthetics.
□ Designer materials made to order through atomic and molecular chemistry. From the rust-free fender to plastic machinery, body replacement parts, and cosmetics.
□ Silicon circuit boards sold by the square inch as plug-in brainpower wherever we go.
□ Plant and farm materials with longer-term yields and longer-term environmental compatibility.
□ New building materials—lightweight, fireproof, thermal, made from solid waste—and the building codes and architecture to go along with them.

The Domain of Micro
□ Computerized satellite telephones.
□ The disappearance of computers in their current form and the emergence of smart desks, smart pens, and smart writing pads. Portability of information access.
□ Our entire life savings registered on a chip on a plastic card in our wallet. Theft proof.
□ Virtual realities that simulate or stimulate anything.

The Domain of Telecommunications
□ Solar-powered global personal communication networks with built-in microchip translation to the language of your choice.
□ Cost-efficient personal video access through high-definition TV in a module the size of a large wallet.
□ Portable pen-driven fax machines the size of a notebook.
□ Open worldwide political forums, trade conferences, educational symposia, etc.—all virtually free for anyone who wants to plug in.

The Domain of the Electronic-Servant House
□ Houses timed, wired, and programmed to turn on or off everything from furnaces and lights to dishwashers, register energy inputs and outputs, order groceries, keep track of family transactions and budgets.

The Domain of Media
□ Top performers available in your own home in 3-D high-definition TV.
□ Voice-activated access to film archives, libraries, news journals, trade association proceedings, etc.

□ Ultrasophisticated simulated vacation environments that make Epcot Center look like a Model T.

□ Music, music, music. Equalized, synthesized, digitized—wherever you want it.

□ The electronic mall—renting a cubicle by the hour and pursuing the world's on-line shopping marketplaces for products and goods, with sales experts on call. Followed by twenty-four-hour global delivery.

□ Classical, pop, or rock concerts—broadcast live or recorded—from any major hall or amphitheater can be received and shown in super-real laser graphics with perfect sound, in auditoriums the size of small movie theaters. Home version available soon.

❖ **Rule of the road:** *Use tec-knowledge to power your career search.*

Technology is not only an element in one's career, it is also the form by which one can navigate one's career. With even a bit of imagination, one can see the interaction of the above technologies with:

□ The way we can build our own capability and performance.

□ The way we can target our careers.

□ The way we discover and learn what needs to be learned.

□ Network possibilities.

□ Discovering our potential.

□ Accessing tactics and game plans.

□ Building resumes.

□ Giving face-to-face interviews by video.

Community career centers, libraries, and placement offices are already providing many of these services.

In Part Two, you will find many ways to apply these technologies to both traditional and untraditional job searches and career management.

Career Map 5:

—☐—

CAREER ENTREPRENEURSHIP

According to James Challenger of Challenger, Gray, and Christmas, Inc., the Chicago outplacement firm, one of the most important trends in employment in the past two decades is the vast rise in the numbers of people who are deserting old career paths for their own small businesses or consultancies.

A flashy idea when it was launched in the 1970s, and one that took on substance in the 1980s, personal entrepreneurism is the career form (or anti-career form) of choice for many. According to Peter Drucker, entrepreneurism means focusing on enhancing the resourcefulness of something. Entrepreneurship is about consciously expanding your tangible value and getting rewarded for it.

In one form, entrepreneurism is an essential part of any career game. Even when he is merely moving from a job in Company A to a job in Company B to a job in Company C, a career voyager is probably operating entrepreneurially—deciding what he has to offer that adds value, constantly upgrading it, and then marketing it in a way that produces maximum personal returns. Those returns, as we've said earlier, include satisfaction *and* a great paycheck.

The level of entrepreneurism can range from practical to explorer's. Practical entrepreneurship involves keeping the radar scanning for targets of opportunity and moving each time the conditions seem right and productive. In explorer's entrepreneurship, you can choose a longer-term strategy and build new trade routes, discover new continents and new cultures, and have the terra firma named for you.

In *The Age of Unreason,* Charles Handy describes organizations as "inverted doughnuts," with a central core surrounded by a solid set of relationships. At the center of the organization the work is being done in a traditional style. In the current phase of organizational evolution we find this core getting more concentrated as the periphery expands enormously. The jobs on the periphery are in no way less important—in fact, they may be the most important in terms of creativity and innovation. The further out from the center, the more entrepreneurial one needs to be. New work rules can be created defining hours, work location, nature of the employment agreement; all sorts of arrangements—including consultancies, part-time work, and performance-based pay—are possible.

With their human resource needs in constant motion, organizations reach out for those skills, talents, trades, and capabilities needed at any given moment. The breakup and reformation of the levels and types of creativity at the far edges of the doughnut is one of the key characteristics of the work world in this decade of transformation.

An entrepreneur is in business for herself. The entrepreneur holds a personal stake in the outcomes of the venture and makes sure that the products and services are consistent with her desires, goals, and vision, as well as her capabilities. When a career voyager/entrepreneur embarks on a new endeavor, she has an inventory of resources already in hand; these can be turned into assets through a little brush-up or training. In addition, career entrepreneurs always keep track of the additional capabilities they need to develop to remain marketable.

Career entrepreneurs must pay special attention to describing themselves as value adders who generate greater value than cost. This can be done through a resume or a consulting brochure, on videotape, or in person. The main thing is that they adapt their language and vocabulary to express themselves in terms of the value added. We cover this in greater detail in Part Two. Deeper than the checklists and inventories, of course, is the need for emotional courage to see life as an opportunity, not a problem. It requires breaking out of boxes and rediscovering the truth about the entrepreneurial and competitive, collaborative nature of the world we live in.

Paradoxically, one early assessment of career entrepreneurship was that everyone was out for themselves. Although that assessment will remain true at some level, the lack of loyalty to the company that we saw in the 1970s and 1980s probably was the best thing that could have happened to many employers and employees caught in the old order. Once people who had been in jobs too long found themselves with pink slips and had to confront despair and disappointment (as painful as that was), many saw what they had been missing in terms of personal freedom and possibility. Many experienced a surge in energy and an enthusiasm for finally being able to do something new. People retiring to "the third half of their lives" (the postcareer years) also discovered the excitement of short-term affiliations as they did only what could maximize their output, results, and rewards in one place after another.

This new attitude represents a sea change in our understanding of what it means to work in a corporation. We are just now adjusting to that. Organizations, products, customers, and employees are a fluid, interconnected, organic system. The employee is not simply the receiver of instructions and the provider of answers, but a more versatile part of the whole. Job security is not an agreement that you can continue doing what you've done for another fifteen years; true job security is the ability to move out and navigate by the stars of fortune—your fortune.

It's frightening that there are thousands of people who worked for many years in large corporations and picked up only a few relevant new skills. They were waiting for the employer to tell them what to do and provide the training to teach them how to do it, rather than using the organization as a massive data base for self-improvement and self-directed career enhancement. A good way to expand your scope as a career entrepreneur is to take on more responsibilities in your job. Rather than minimize what's expected, maximize it. Look for new things to take on, people to meet, task teams to be a part of, afterwork discussion groups to join, and new material to read.

Handy refers to the need for a "skills portfolio." You want both breadth and depth in any good portfolio. You want to have lots of valuable assets of learning, knowledge, skills, qualities, capabilities, courses taken, accomplishments won. You want to keep your portfolio active and alive. Maintaining a good career portfolio requires that you continually get input from the outside world; otherwise, it's all too easy to get stuck in a rut and constantly rejustify the work that we've been doing. More on this in Part Two.

A restraint to career entrepreneurism is the old idea that it's impolite to brag. Many of us have had our spirit smacked down in early life by teachers, family, or others who told us we were stupid or slow or didn't have the right stuff. Don't believe it. You've got the right stuff—go ahead and flaunt it. If you *don't* have the right stuff, go out and get it and then flaunt it!

Participation in the work environment at a variety of levels is essential to career entrepreneurism. Associate with groups that are not necessarily connected to your current position. Flavor your social activities with creative types, straight types, and non-types. Avoid the trap of palling around only with those in your field whom you have known the longest. Travel—both mentally and geographically—to places you haven't seen.

Like other approaches to life, career entrepreneurship can be learned. Examining these propositions for the first time is enough to get the game going. We have seen that when people finally had it with the companies they'd worked for for twenty or more years, they were able—with the right coaching and counseling—to shuck off the old ideas and beliefs about job title, refresh their self-assessment, repackage their capabilities, and launch themselves into new endeavors. Part Two describes how to do this.

❖ **Rule of the road:** *Be open to experimentation.*

If you've just graduated or if you have been in a job for a short time, experiment (tactfully). If you don't have a job now, go on interviews in fields totally different from yours. Try to write your resume in a way that presents something new and valuable about yourself. Remember that one law of free-market economics is nothing ventured, nothing gained. Read a book on a subject you know nothing about. What might first seem like jargon might emerge as an idea that you can understand and elaborate on. Ask questions; consult references. Stay open to picking up information about someone else's field, nose around in it, read product brochures, talk to salespeople— experiment in every way you can. As a career entrepreneur you are your own R & D department.

❖ **Rule of the road:** *Get advice from others.*

Ask successful people you know (or who your friends know) about their careers. Find out what they're reading and what they believe. Find out what jobs they held on their way to the present post, and what they found most useful in these positions. Look for the things you don't know and be willing to ask "stupid" questions. Asking questions is the way to success.

❖ **Rule of the road:** *Bring work and life together.*

As a career entrepreneur, you no longer have a nine-to-five, five-days-a-week job. Your work stretches through every part of your activity. This is worthwhile only if the work you gain also provides you with a certain amount of excitement, adventure, and pleasure. Look creatively at how to adjust family time and work time and at how to work at home or abroad or from your RV. Discuss your spouse's job field and career path with him or her; explore the possibility of how the two of you might work together in years to come. Be clear about what compromises you and your family are willing to make, and for how long. Make sure you include all of your family and your support network in your decisions.

❖ **Rule of the road:** *Build networks.*

For the savvy career entrepreneur there is no such thing as idle conversation. Everyone you meet and everywhere you go presents you with an opportunity to conduct some benign espionage into what's happening in the work world. If you vacation in Brussels, spend a few days sipping beer in the Grand' Place, then seek out some European businesspeople and learn about their ways of working and their contacts. Step up and speak to someone at a gallery opening or community fund-raiser. Look for people who look like they're having fun in life and find out how they're doing it.

❖ **Rule of the road:** *Find and use mentors.*

A pilot meets you as you come into a narrow harbor and directs you through the unknown rocks and shoals. A mentor is a person who does that with your career. Find someone who is already successful who could be committed to your success. This person should be willing to coach you and give you accurate feedback and support. Good mentors are hard to find, but they are out there. Avoid people who agree with you too frequently; instead, look for those who challenge your thinking. Welcome critical reviews.

❖ **Rule of the road:** *Support others.*

You're not going to get very far if you cut off your support system or don't acknowledge it fully. A wise counselor once said that you need to give out as much good advice as you take in. Don't simply be the recipient of good ideas and feedback—look for ways to establish relationships that are empowering to others. If you know two or three others who are in a similar position, consider forming a support team to meet occasionally for a few hours to share information about opportunities, barriers, and tactics. Make these relationships not a conspiracy of mediocrity but a conspiracy of self-development, capability, and performance ability.

❖ **Rule of the road:** *Keep personal purpose and vision in sight.*

It's tough to market a product when you're not really sure what it does or what it's worth. Most of us have a favorite airline, a favorite car maker, and perhaps even a favorite grocery store. We have a sense of what those companies stand for, and we can probably explain why we do business with them. When we come to our own professional life, too few of us clearly express who we are, where we're going, and what qualities or skills we have to contribute. In clarifying a purpose or mission for your life and work you have a real opportunity to distinguish yourself from the crowd. Spend necessary energy to answer the question: What is a way of working and living that would produce the greatest satisfaction and self-development for me? Or, ask a question of your own. Continually clarify your purpose.

Practice communicating your purpose and commitments to family and close friends. Keep developing and clarifying as you go. Such a grounding not only allows you to make more effective judgments of what behaviors and activities are important, it also ensures that you have a powerful communications platform to others who need to know what you're about.

An entrepreneur must be in touch with the rewards and the cost of the work. Look for the psychic and material rewards that you want and need. By enhancing value, you enhance return. If you need to earn more money, you need to be able to deliver more value and let people know about it (salary-negotiating strategies are shown in Part Two). The quest for personal growth is consistent with expanding the safety and sanity of the planet, and the spirit of entrepreneurism is at the heart of a lively career.

Part Two

THE HIDDEN JOB MARKET

The hidden job market is the vast underlying reservoir of job opportunity that lies, like an emerging continent, a few inches beneath the surface of the day-to-day interchange in career futures that most of us are so inexorably tied to. It is the source of career possibilities that extend far beyond the limited horizons most of us have set for our job lives.

The hidden job market, like many marketplaces in the knowledge age, is as much a network of ideas and approaches as it is of tangible job postings. This is the world of possibilities which, though far greater in scope than the tangible exchanges of the help-wanted ads, is less visible to the unaided eye.

The hidden job market is a fabric of invention and problem solving that is limited only by the scope of the population that passes over it. It is where job opportunity comes from in the first place.

The fundamental proposition of the hidden job market is that jobs originate in the unfilled needs of a dynamic society, and that in a complex world, much of what needs to be done is not obvious on the first pass. Jobs in the hidden job market take many forms: from the announced retirement which in a few weeks will need a replacement candidate to the product on the drawing boards that will need a champion and then a project manager, and then a few hundred production types followed by more smart career entrepreneurs.

One of the basic facts that define the hidden job market is the fact that some 80 percent of the jobs available on any given day are not advertised, and that there is always preliminary activity which is very open weeks, months, or seasons before a job is announced publicly.

In addition to preempting the flow of career information to the public markets, the career voyager mastering the hidden job market learns to anticipate the movements of technology, businesses, and consumer needs. She is the captain of the enterprise, and the designer of her own future.

To know how the hidden job market works is to know how society is moving. To participate in it in a very practical way is to follow the guidelines and techniques laid out in this action-oriented section of the book.

What follows is a set of instructions for mastering the hidden job market.

HOW TO USE THIS PART OF THE BOOK

□

You can read through this part of the book taking the action steps along the way or you can simply familiarize yourself with the process and then go back the second time and use the book as an action plan.

Either way is all right with us. We will, however, assume that each step along the way is being put into practice as you go along. Between the chapter on interviewing and that on follow-up, for example, we will assume that you put the book down and went out and had the interviews, and will speak to you about follow-up as though several interviews have been held.

Probably it is best to skim the book first, stopping with bookmarks to note the next actions you want to take, and then as the career voyage takes hold, to go back and use each chapter to guide you directly.

So the voice you will hear from us will be from the point of view that you have been active in your job campaign.

1

---□---

THE VOYAGE OF
SELF-DISCOVERY

Our initial aim in this second part of the book is to set the stage for the full-size payoffs that await you when you put personal truth ahead of practical-compromise matters.

Many of us have been mistakenly convinced that success requires continual adaptation to external situations and circumstances and that *not* to adapt is to be seen as a maverick or misfit. This conviction is especially strong in tough financial times or in highly bureaucratic organizations where the "good" worker does the job under the most rigid or stifling conditions, and the one who doesn't play by the rules is not considered a team player.

This "conform or else" mind-set was founded on ideas fostered in the late nineteenth century. The industrial models developed then, which were essentially dictatorial and dominating, were the most efficient way to meet the demands of the machine. Doing what you were told *was* the work ethic, and most schools hastened to teach it and most parents to espouse it. These "theory X" notions of work-style control—in which employees and employers see one another as basically untrustworthy—still pervades the management psyche of developed and developing industries, economies and nations. However, they cannot hold together successfully in these times when teamwork is used to grapple with the complexities of organizational life.

Despite the great gains in recognition of worker participation, career choice, empowerment, and self-development, when the going gets tough, the old cast-iron shadows of "a hard day's work for a day's pay" still tend to clamp down on our thinking about what work is and can be. The old view is that work is supposed to hurt. We support the view that you do best at those things you love, and that personal satisfaction, capability, and the ability to be versatile and flexible are fundamental to successful work—good times or bad.

The hidden job market is found among jobs based on newly created possibilities, not "slots" that need filling; it is about the kinds of work opportunities that are rarely advertised in the help wanteds. In this section we propose a series of strategies and ideas based on the premise that work and life are interconnected. You must start from your strongest interests and talents.

The next several chapters are devoted to finding out something new about yourself. You will discover more about who you really are beneath the job titles, roles, and degrees. You will look at your life from new vantage points and find new answers to the old question What do I want to do when I grow up?

It is important to pay attention to the instructions and give honest replies to the questions asked, whether they have an obvious connection to the job world or not. There will be times when you will want to make your answers fit preexisting or comfortable descriptions or labels or to tailor your answers to past successes. Doing that will only reinforce the conventional view of the situation, to the detriment of a bigger and better approach.

Think about:

How do you feel about your coming work week? Imagine yourself on a Monday morning heading to work. Check any of the phrases or statements that you associate with the idea of going to work. If you don't have a job now, make your selections based on your last job.

_____ If I only had a job, then I'd be happy

_____ Numb

_____ Nervous

_____ I like my work better than weekends

_____ Sick—the economy worries me

_____ Scared

_____ Anxious—I'm looking for my first job

_____ It's 8:00 A.M. I'm a night person

_____ I wish I'd gone to college

_____ Fifty-fifty—it's not all bad

_____ I should be making more money

_____ It's a pleasure

_____ I love my work

_____ I need a change

_____ No complaints

_____ It's drudgery

_____ There must be more to life

_____ I feel like a cog

_____ I wish it were Friday

_____ Successful

_____ Rotten

_____ Bored

_____ Powerful

_____ Trapped

_____ I hate it

_____ My job is my life

_____ I like the people I work
with

_____ Charged up

_____ I'm afraid of more layoffs

_____ Is this why I went to
college?

_____ I need more training

_____ Help!

_____ Stale

_____ Fulfilled

_____ My job's convenient

_____ A chimp could do better

_____ I make good money

_____ My boss gets the credit

_____ The bills have to be paid

_____ You heard of Black
Monday?

Add any additional feelings you can think of about your most current work
or job:

_____

_____

_____

_____

_____

Many people confuse their feelings about *work* with their feelings about their
job. The two are not identical. The answers we've gotten to thousands of
questionnaires prove this. As we expected, the most frequent responses were
often the cliché, shorthand answers people give when they are suspicious,
guarded, or defensive about revealing their feelings, even to themselves.

For instance, a middle-level executive in a pharmaceutical company said,
"I wouldn't do it if I didn't like it." However, an in-depth interview revealed
that the statement had very little to do with the actual work of his work
week. What he really enjoyed about his *job* were the trips in the company
plane, a schedule that permitted him a lot of time out of the office, and, of
course, the salary and prestige.

There was much direct negativity: "Rotten" or "I wish it were Friday."
Here, too, people didn't always know what it was they actually hated. For
example, the statement "I wish it were Friday" was later amplified by Harold
M., a market researcher, into, "My boss is a tyrant; I can't ever do anything

right." Harold's adverse relationship to his boss, though certainly important, is actually only a secondary aspect of his work. His actual *work* is market research, which he likes so much that he often voluntarily works at home on weekends. He wishes it were Friday so he can get away from his boss—*not from his work.*

JOBS AND WORK

□

It is common to confuse ideas about the job—the set of responsibilities that keep us solvent and, sometimes, indentured—with questions about the work itself. Career voyagers know the difference. Most people, when answering questions about work, usually spoke about their *job* and its fair or foul impact on them. Their *work* was not considered much, except in professional or technical occupations, where the deepest levels of the distinction were not very obvious.

In fact, work and job have vastly different meanings. The *job* is the environment within which a human being does his or her *work*. Webster's definition of *work*, originating in the nineteenth century and subscribed to by millions of people is "The exertion of physical or mental energy toward some purpose or end; the matter on which one is employed." In other words, work is what you are hired to do for those who hire you.

However, there is a fresher, freer meaning of work. Erich Fromm, the eminent psychoanalyst, pointed out that satisfying work and love are a person's healthiest outlets for creative life and the prime source of all his or her pleasure energy. Work is what humankind *does* on the planet. It embraces us at almost all of the basic levels: survival, physical and mental energies, relationships, service, knowledge base, the thirst for learning, the need to contribute to the planet, play, purpose, and more.

In earlier days people had a powerful relationship to work. Families and communities were based on interlocking social and economic activities that connected them in a common cause. Later, job titles, position, commercial hierarchies, bargained wage scales and subdivision of labor took hold, as did the routines of the mechanical, industrial, and commercial situations and the question What's your job? Thus, simple work degenerated into simplistic tasks in an overly complex commercial enterprise. Having the right job, virtually despite the work it entailed, became the thing to go for.

Repressing one's need for personally satisfying *work* because of a fear of not having the right *job* invites physical and mental trouble. Your needs for deep personal accomplishment and relevant self-expression can't be stored away in mothballs. Having the right work to do and the ability to refocus the direction of that work sustains mental and physical well-being. This ability to change course and destination is essential for the career voyager. Medical studies have shown that people who stay in work that they don't like out of fear, habit, or stubbornness can suffer from stress, fatigue, substance abuse, and other medical problems. A kind of personal midcareer vertigo is another result.

All this attention to *work itself* is not intended to bypass the importance of the *job*. All manner of advantages or features of a job can matter very much. These are *job benefits*, and they include:

□ *Your compensation package.* Base salary and bonuses, pension plans, profit sharing, insurance, and other forms of compensation.
□ *The status you get.* Personal self-esteem is affected by many tangible and intangible factors, such as office location, job title, prestige, and power. The status arising from the position will also reflect on community standing, peer groups, and social relationships outside of work; it often has a ripple effect on your spouse and children. As we strive for greater personal freedom, the demands of job status might present social obligations that outweigh the benefits.
□ *Job style.* The hours, flexible work schedules, dress code, education and training opportunities, vacation policies, expense account, convenience of the job location, the climate, work-space design, level and range of travel, amiability of co-workers; in short, a whole mix of tangibles and intangibles can enhance or ruin a job experience for you.
□ *Job security.* Your feeling that your job (or your relationship to the company) will continue for as long as you wish provides an important foundation for your sense of well-being and the predictability of your endeavors. However, in an age of uncertainty, true job security is a myth. In the past, fear of the uncertain has been one of the most powerful forces keeping people locked into jobs that bored them or gave them that sinking feeling with each new work week. People have endured the trials of inept bosses, sexual harassment, sixty-hour work weeks, and other indignities in order to feel that they can count on job security.

In recent years, from high flyers on Wall Street to low rollers in manufacturing, workers have seen their so-called job security evaporate in the face of corporate indiscretion, mergers, cost-cutting purges, and a dozen other organizational distresses. True job security is a mirage.

❖ **Rule of the road:** *Stay loose.*

Your best job security is to keep constantly in touch with your improving skills and deepening interests and with the multiple ways you can relate to the changing world and maintain personal satisfaction.

WORK SATISFACTION

□

Finding work that produces the deepest sense of gratification, participation, and satisfaction is a fundamental right. Once the social neuroses of materialism and success are stripped away, it's also clear that having such work is a basic human drive.

❖ **Rule of the Road:** *For the open mind there are open doors.*

For those who have been on their career voyages for some time, a small but strong voice tells them not to invest too heavily in the concept of work pleasure. The idea of an imaginative, user-friendly way of working seems interesting, but not quite practical enough.

The aim of these next chapters is to get you engaged in a passionate pilgrimage through ideas and strategies for reframing the work idea from one of practical necessity to one of chosen vocation. The rewards for this kind of thinking are good: working for personal gain while gaining personal worth.

To achieve the kind of work or job that provides financial *and* psychological rewards requires only a natural shift of thinking and attitude. It doesn't require a cultural leap of great dimensions. As you will see as you work through these pages, those aspects of working life that hold pleasure and psychic rewards for you might not be attractive to others. We are looking for the right mixtures of variables.

In these chapters, you will be invited to do a number of exercises to help you weigh in on the scales of opportunity and organize, suggest, or define the parameters of your personal career success. *Please do the work suggested.* Some of the exercises might seem simplistic or obvious, but our experience has taught us that it is only when we take the trouble to look beyond the obvious and to challenge old assumptions that we expose our greatest potential.

The next exercise focuses on correlating work pleasure and job benefits on your career voyage.

YOUR JOB ANALYSIS

1. Thinking about how you relate to work and job, read through the list of characteristics and cross out any values that are not important to you. Add any others we haven't thought of.
2. Consider how much each remaining value is being rewarded in your current (or most recent) work. Assign a number from 1 (low) to 5 (high) in the column labeled Now to quantify this.
3. Decide which values you would like to stress more in future jobs. Check the ten items that would be most important to you in the Future column.

Characteristics	Now	Future
Chance for advancement		
Having more choice in what I do		
Having a better work space or office		
Having longer vacations		
Working on a team		
Having more authority		
Supervising (more) people		
Working at home more		
Doing more physical work		

Characteristics	Now	Future
Doing independent thinking		
Making policy decisions		
Being supervised well		
Having a secretary or clerical support		
Carrying out policy decisions		
Meeting people outside my office		
More personal self-expression		
Dressing casually		
Working with high tech equipment		
Flexible hours		
Traveling		
Learning more		
Chance to become partner or officer		
Profit sharing		
Lack of pressure		
Freedom to try new things		
Pay raises based primarily on results		
Convenient job location		

Characteristics	Now	Future
Congenial co-workers		
A company car		
A bigger benefit package		
Smaller company		
More variety		
More security		

We suspect that as you responded you had a few pangs and nagging concerns about what has been missing in your work. The main point in this exercise is not getting right or wrong answers, but expanding your sense of what you want to have in future jobs. If this was accomplished, move on. If you want to work over the ideas of work values, come back to this part as you develop job targets in future exercises.

❖ **Rule of the road:** *Seek equilibrium.*

We'll conclude this chapter with the story of someone who has developed a happy balance between work pleasures and job benefits.

Hal Brook works in an exotic plant greenhouse on Long Island, New York. He knows a lot about work pleasure. When we asked him our opening question, "How do you feel about the coming work week?" he said, "Fine. Why not?" As we found out, during in-depth interviewing, his actual situation was as true as his words. On both levels of his job—work pleasure and almost all job benefits—Hal was in equilibrium.

Hal's *work* was his primary pleasure. He said, "I like growing plants and working with living things. I like the way they smell. Just looking at them makes me feel good. . . . I like taking care of them. Plants are a lot more beautiful than many people. And they don't talk back."

Hal's job benefits were a mixed bag. He said things like "I get up at 5 A.M. But I like it, so it's OK. . . . I don't like waiting on customers but sometimes I have to. It's part of the job . . . . I hate business suits and I don't have to wear them. . . . I'm able to use my studies in bio-genetics and agronomy to help produce new and astonishingly beautiful flowers nobody has ever seen before. . . . I don't make as much money as I would if I worked for a big company, but I like it here. . . . And my boss is an OK guy."

If you enjoy what you do for a living, you are bound to do it better—thus creating greater economic value. If you know who you are, then you will fit better into a career *you can design for yourself.* Unless you are one in a million who can't fit in *anywhere,* there is a career or job target for you that will provide equilibrium. All you have to do is know who and what you are and how to find where you fit.

In the next chapter we're going to help you take a closer look at your own personal pleasures. Then we will help you see how to translate these personal pleasures into work pleasures and a work direction that suits you.

2

PERSONAL
WORK PLEASURE

WHAT I (WOULD) LIKE TO DO

Let's start with an exercise. Please put a check mark beside those statements below that apply to you. Feel free to modify the statements or add more if you think of an item we didn't list. Indicate things you may not have tried yet by including the word *would*. Go through the list from your heart, not your mind; you don't have to connect the things you like to do to a particular job. That will come later. For now simply list what you might like to do if you could.

_____ I (would) like making deals
_____ I (would) like teaching
_____ I (would) like playing music
_____ I (would) like working with computers
_____ I (would) like strategy games
_____ I (would) like foreign travel
_____ I (would) like composing music
_____ I (would) like entertaining

_____ I (would) like collecting
_____ I (would) like restoring (e.g., furniture, jewelry)
_____ I (would) like backpacking
_____ I (would) like training groups
_____ I (would) like consulting
_____ I (would) like verbal interactions
_____ I (would) like working with money

_____ I (would) like sales work
_____ I (would) like research
_____ I (would) like supervising others
_____ I (would) like flying
_____ I (would) like gardening
_____ I (would) like taking care of others
_____ I (would) like coaching
_____ I (would) like technology
_____ I (would) like catering parties
_____ I (would) like serious art tours
_____ I (would) like meeting new people
_____ I (would) like fishing
_____ I (would) like learning languages
_____ I (would) like making home videos
_____ I (would) like teaching kids
_____ I (would) like family counseling
_____ I (would) like working alone
_____ I (would) like to sing and/or dance
_____ I (would) like making presentations
_____ I (would) like writing ads
_____ I (would) like cabinetry
_____ I (would) like making order out of chaos
_____ I (would) like being in informal surroundings
_____ I (would) like designing clothes

_____ I (would) like solving organizational problems
_____ I (would) like negotiating
_____ I (would) like interviewing
_____ I (would) like politics
_____ I (would) like working with numbers
_____ I (would) like nursing
_____ I (would) like building physical structures
_____ I (would) like organizing events
_____ I (would) like sports
_____ I (would) like international affairs
_____ I (would) like producing events
_____ I (would) like bringing people together
_____ I (would) like leading tours
_____ I (would) like routine orderly tasks
_____ I (would) like a secure position
_____ I (would) like freedom to do my own thing
_____ I (would) like taking care of children
_____ I (would) like intellectual endeavors
_____ I (would) like cooking
_____ I (would) like running my own show
_____ I (would) like taking risks
_____ I (would) like creative work
_____ I (would) like a big company
_____ I (would) like counseling

_____ I (would) like public relations

_____ I (would) like designing systems

_____ I (would) like writing

_____ I (would) like public appearances

_____ I (would) like leading meetings

_____ I (would) like analyzing

_____ I (would) like problem solving

_____ I (would) like working at home part- or full-time

_____ I (would) like dabbling in the stock market

_____ I (would) like working hard for big goals

_____ I (would) like writing for television

_____ I (would) like intricate work

_____ I (would) like leading a team

_____ I (would) like being well known

_____ I (would) like_____

_____ I (would) like_____

_____ I (would) like_____

_____ I (would) like_____

_____ I (would) like_____

_____ I (would) like_____

Look back over the list. How may items did you check?_____

Narrow down the list to your top ten. List them below:

My top personal interests:

1. _____
2. _____
3. _____
4. _____
5. _____
6. _____
7. _____
8. _____
9. _____
10. _____

Consider this a warm-up and a loosening up of the pleasure principle. You might have told yourself that this was an irrelevant exercise. What am I doing checking off gardening or strategy games when what I really need to do is get to *work*? Is it relevant to explore the world of personal pleasures when beginning an examination of potential, productive work? Emphatically, we say *yes*.

It is because so little real thinking about personal desires and interests has gone into job choices that exercises like this can build a lifeline to long-term satisfaction that pays big dividends. People tend to see things in black and white; so you might think, Yes, scuba is great fun on vacation, but . . . be realistic, it's not going to pay off in the long run as a job for me because . . . And before the thought has run its course, you are gripped by the practical realities of how you are going to raise the family, build the college fund, buy your dream house, and so on. The quest for personal satisfaction through work goes against conventional job-security wisdom.

Listen to Indiana Schuer confess her deep conflicts about her position as an office manager for an international consulting company based in the Midwest:

> Yes the pay is OK, and my boss is thoughtful; we take turns making the coffee, and I'm learning how to do the finances. In this small business I know I am learning skills that will serve me well in future companies I might want to join, but it hurts to think about going on this way forever. Why did I study art history for four years? And when I spend a weekend reading Racine or Molière, I feel so mundane coming in to the office to send faxes that I could scream. When I hear the top managers talk about discovering a new gallery that I already know by heart, I ask myself: Do they know or even respect my liberal education? I'm not wired to be a businesswoman, and yet here I am depending on the paycheck like everyone else. I'm in a box, and I know it. I don't want to grow into a consultant, and I don't want to become an office machine.

Indiana made some simple discoveries. Six months after an initial counseling session, she was working at another job: assistant to a woman who was opening a local art gallery. The money was less, but the personal rewards (the psychic pay) were so much higher. Her conventional business skills were of great use to the new employer, and her liberal arts background made her feel quite at home in a new occupation and a new perspective. "I don't understand why I didn't think of this in the first place," she said. "I guess that the people who think they know what you should do with your life don't see the full picture. In my case it was my ever practical mom and my college placement office. They want me to be successful, but they have a limited view: mostly practical—wages and growth potential. The risks are greater where I am now, but so are the rewards. I'm not turning my back on the quality of my work life again."

*   *   *

Now, try this test. Go back to page 42—how you felt when you went to work—and reconsider the list of statements. This time when you respond, do so in relation to how you feel about your work itself—not the job benefits. You may find that all your answers do not still apply. If not, make the appropriate changes.

Now, choose the most meaningful statement. In the space below, in clear, plainspoken terms, write a statement of 50 words or less that explains why you feel the way you do about your most recent work.

My most meaningful statement is:

_____

_____

_____

_____

I feel that way because:

_____

_____

_____

_____

Reread what you wrote. On balance, are you getting enough personal *pleasure*—not just job benefits—out of your work? Don't fake—this is a key question; one that's important because it touches on a vital issue: how you spend the largest chunk of your time.

YOUR 10,000 DAYS—AN ADVENTURE OR A DRAG?

Life is long and rich. Yet you have probably never calculated that the average eight-hour-a-day job occupies 10,000 days of your most productive years. The amount of time you spend on a job is more than is often spent in marriage, in family life, in school, or in many other organized human activities.

We have inherited cultural, religious, and practical barriers or boxes to the idea of personal satisfaction being part of our day-to-day work. We are often driven by peer pressure and family demands. For many of us, the Calvinist or Protestant work ethic is so deeply embedded that it seems vaguely immoral to acknowledge the deeply felt satisfactions of self-expression. These guilts are strengthened by the marketplace and by the materialistic agendas many of us get caught up in—those bills do need to be paid.

What are some of the inner assumptions, opinions, and beliefs that could keep you from weaving the pleasure principle into your own career track? List them below.

_____

_____

_____

_____

_____

If you wrote comments such as:

I have a job now that I hate, but I don't know how to find one that's more fun.

OR

I don't like what I do as much as some of the interests I checked, but I don't know if I could do any of those things well enough to get paid for it.

OR

I think I know now what I like to do, but I don't have a clue as to how to get work doing it.

OR

I'm afraid. What if I can't do well what I like to do?

OR

In today's job market I'm lucky to have anything.

You can see how traditional thinking might hold you in the grip of an old view of work.

Personal Payoff

You now know something truly worth knowing about yourself—your ten most important interests. Given the right orientation, these interests can expand into job possibilities you've possibly never thought of before.

In the 1990s, there are over 110 million jobs in this country. Given the inherent dynamics of the economy, every year a minimum of 15 percent of these jobs turn over—more than 17 million job changes a year. Not only is there a turnover in old jobs, but in an age of diversity, new *kinds* of jobs replace old ones as fast as MTV videos replace one another. Even in most recessions, hundreds of thousands of *new* jobs are added to the economy annually. In this environment, the only reasons not to find yourself truly sustaining work are confused thinking and a lack of organized effort.

Your perfect new job could have been vacated yesterday at 3:00 P.M. Or perhaps it exists in the mind of an employer who doesn't realize how much he or she needs your brand of problem solving. The right jobs are there—*you* need to find them. But before we can show you how to locate those jobs, we must be certain we are speaking to the true you.

We are escalating now from interest to pleasure. Start thinking, wishing, daydreaming, remembering what gives you true pleasure. Pleasure is different from "interest." As we define it, an interest is intrinsically attractive to you, but the pursuit of it is active and usually fairly structured. The pleasures we speak of now are more amorphous, unstructured, spontaneous, peripheral. These pleasures can be active or passive. They do not necessarily involve "doing" (although they may). Think of these pleasures without any reference to the work you do now, or to work you'd like to do. Let your mind free-associate as you fill in the lines below. Remember, pleasure can make sense or nonsense, and it can have a purpose or be purposeless.

In the following paragraphs we use the term *mind* to describe the intellectual pleasures of thinking, learning, studying, interpreting, and appreciating. We use the term *body* to describe physical excitements that relate to dancing, sports, manual labor, music, and sensuality. Then there are those pleasures, by far the widest category of all, that affect many aspects of our self—mind, body, and spirit.

YOUR PLEASURE PROFILE—PART I

□

In this section you will find eight rather arbitrary types of mind-body pleasures. In each category, after reading our example, describe something that would give you pleasure. Don't worry if what you say in one category overlaps others.

Physical Pleasures

Examples: Exercising, sports, performing (e.g., dancing, singing), hiking, running, working with hands, home repair, building things, boating, contact sports, and gardening.

Tony Bellow: "I don't much like home repair work or any of that stuff. I like sports. I'm a very good athlete. Well-coordinated. I like to keep my body on the edge, press my coordination and balance."

_____

_____

_____

_____

_____

Sensual Pleasures

Examples: Eating, smelling, seeing, hearing, and touching.

Sarah Dunes: "I love colors. I can see a wall color in my head, and I can match fabrics, floors, and lighting. I don't need a swatch or anything. I know the right colors to match instantly."

_____

_____

_____

_____

_____

Intellectual Pleasures

Examples: Reading, studying, researching, analyzing, organizing, problem solving, decision making, and planning.

> Bryn Thorn: I like researching projects and analyzing subjects, but I must say I don't like the responsibility of making the decision. That would keep me up nights."

_____

_____

_____

_____

_____

Creative and Aesthetic Pleasures

Examples: Painting, composing, writing, designing, acting, crafts, collecting art and art objects, sewing, and cooking.

> Phil Spring: "I like inventing learning environments, spaces from which people can see beyond the obvious to new possibilities. I can do training rooms, playgrounds, and a high-tech, high-touch computer laboratory."

_____

_____

_____

_____

_____

Interpersonal Pleasures

Examples: Meeting people, talking to people, learning about people, understanding people, helping, teaching, participating in teamwork, competing.

> Heidi Fuches: "I get energized by having to organize high-powered events: a shareholders' meeting by video, for example. I enjoy negotiating face-to-face or by phone. I like solo presentations."

_____
_____
_____
_____
_____

Communication Pleasures

Examples: Contacting people, persuading people, arguing with people, negotiating or bargaining, explaining ideas, and getting one's point across.

June Easter: "Not for me. I prefer to have other people do the bargaining for me. I think I tend to be too agreeable and always want to keep peace."

_____
_____
_____
_____
_____

Mechanical Pleasures

Examples: Operating interactive video computers, building a system or structure, designing production processes.

Brenda Assum: "I love to have the opportunity to be involved in the layout of production processes, distribution systems. To bring the mechanical and human factors together."

_____
_____
_____
_____

Emotional Climate Conditions

Examples: Optimistic, pessimistic, risk taker, cautious, fast temper, slow fuse, enjoy challenge, enjoy conformity, like change, like routine.

Harry Garrick: "I like to know where everything is. Even my shoehorn. I find unexpected change very upsetting."

_____

_____

_____

_____

Your Pleasure Profile—Part II

Take as much time as necessary to give accurate answers to the following questions.

1. Who would you like to be if you weren't yourself?
   _____

2. If you were working a three-day work week, what would you do with the remaining four days?
   _____
   _____

3. List the three places and climates you find most enjoyable.
   _____
   _____

4. What do your closest friends like most about you?
   _____
   _____

5. What do you like most about yourself?
   _____
   _____

6. What is your most secret pleasure?
   _____
   _____

7. What are your favorite tools?
   _____
   _____

8. What kind of person do you find most attractive?
   _____
   _____

9. When you meet people for the first time, what would you like them to think about you?

_____

_____

10. Looking back over the past five years, list the three events or occasions you were personally involved in that gave you the most pleasure.

_____

_____

_____

_____

_____

_____

Now, go back and reconsider your list of top ten interests on page 53. Do they still hold? Look again at both parts of your Pleasure Profile. Does it stand up on a second reading? Is it you? If something troubles you, *change it*. As you travel through this book, you will be constantly revising and adjusting your answers to make them correspond more accurately with the discoveries you make about yourself and your potential.

Put an asterisk in front of your top five interests.

PERSONAL PLEASURE SUMMARY
□

In 100 words or less, describe yourself in terms of what pleases, interests, motivates, provides pleasures, and rewards you.

_____

_____

_____

_____

In chapter 1, we asked you to tell yourself some of the feelings you have about going to work. These feelings represented the bottom line of your job attitude, the product of the positive and negative aspects of your work. In this chapter you saw those activities that interest you and give you pleasure. In the next chapter we show you how to begin to free yourself from the tyranny of rigid career thinking.

3

---□---

HELP WANTED

What's wrong with these classified ads?

RESEARCH WRITER   fee paid $24,000
MA + 2 yrs qualitative experience including ability to deal
effectively w/others. Sm bkgrnd industry studies req. Fast
growing co. Good benefits.
Call Mr. Matthews 555-3218.

SOFTWARE EDITOR   fee paid $28,000
Assistant to software creative designer. Experience with
games and instructional materials essential.
Call Ms. Barrow 555-2904.

RECYCLING COORDINATOR
To manage entire community recycling program of Western
Ulster County. Beginning June 1992. Experience essential.
Salary range $20,000 to $26,000 depending on experience.
Contact Ms. Grimaldi 555-2221 extension 453.

Help wanted ads are hazy and imprecise. Job titles often describe only one or
two aspects of the job, and those are sometimes the least important ones in
terms of what you finally do and what's in it for you. Job descriptions leave

out many important details and include irrelevant information. You need to be able to interpret these employment listings to get more mileage from this job-market source.

Most classified writers describe the title and apparent function, leaving it to the reader to check his skills against those listed. The assumption is that the listed skills, degrees, and experience track is *the* way to get the job done. Other possible approaches to accomplishing the job are not considered. Going beyond the small print, so to speak, will give you a tremendous advantage in understanding and answering help wanted ads—if you must. We say *must* since, as you know by now, most of the best jobs don't ever get advertised. That's what the hidden job market is all about.

Think about what want ads really are. They are the last resort of the company that hasn't attracted applicants by word of mouth. One has to wonder about this. Why use the newspaper to offer a job when a few telephone calls to a good school or a word to a friend could achieve equal or better results?

Nonetheless, here's what you can get out of want ads: You can learn a lot about yourself by writing them.

❖ Rule of the Road: *You are not a job title.*

Like many others, you may have been brainwashed to believe that people gain their identity through their job titles or positions. When someone asks you what you do, you say, "I'm an editor," "I'm a computer programmer," "I'm a psychologist," or "I'm a model maker."

However, you are *not* your job title. You have a collection of skills, potentials, educated guesses, personality, talents, physical endowments, and desires. You are a person who can and does earn a living and who lives a life that is evolving. If all of your characteristics have been stuffed uneasily into a box called "job title" that you now accept as part of your identity, there is a strong element of self-deception or blindness that lowers your chances of achieving a greatly successful career voyage.

Let's go back and reconsider the three want ads at the beginning of this chapter.

RESEARCH WRITER AD

Can you tell what the research writer job really requires from reading the ad? Here's the transcript of our investigation at the office of the man who posted this listing.

Q: *At the opening of the ad you list first a master's degree and two years' experience. Are these both essential requirements?*

A: When you get right down to it—maybe not, I guess. There's nothing magic about a master's , or even the two years' experience really. But we received so many responses the last time we ran the ad, I decided to be more particular this time to cut down the interviewing load.

Q: *What's really required then?*

A: Good clear writing of a particular type—writing that can deal with technical data, statistics, figures, and conclusions and that can make a complicated subject come across clearly and understandably.

Q: *What's the subject matter?*

A: It varies. The company does a variety of research projects for industry. Mostly the work is done in the area of utilization of materials, testing for various characteristics of materials, such as metal crystallization, stress, corrosion—that sort of thing.

Q: *How are these reports prepared by the writer?*

A: There's always a project engineer responsible for each project. He accumulates all the data, comes up with the conclusions, organizes the elements of the report; then he meets with the writer for a day or two, going over the information. Then the writer puts together a rough draft; the engineer then reviews it to make sure it is accurate. The writer does a finished version that is approved by the engineer and by one of the partners of the firm.

Q: *So what you really need is a writer who can work with technical terms and data and make it understandable. If such a person got in to see you—but didn't have an M.A.—would you consider him or her?*

A: I think I would. As a matter of fact, our best writer has a B.S. in engineering and no prior job experience—he's straight out of school. But he really knows how to get the ideas across and that solve the problem. He's completely upgraded the quality of the reports.

Conclusion

Job titles and descriptions usually hide as much as they reveal. They can be misleading and paralyzing. They may prevent you from applying. But if something about the ad catches you, and you can overcome your hesitation and decide to make a try, some investigation might reveal the *hidden opportunities* in the ad.

SOFTWARE EDITOR AD

□

The software editor job is an example of an ad that says almost nothing. What, for instance, does *editor* mean in this context? We explored the actual requirements for this job.

Q: *How much programming—if any—is there in this job?*

A: Not more than an hour a day. If that. It's mainly like a word-processing editor. Or an editor of instructional materials.

Q: *Does this person have to be as savvy with computer games as a Nintendo-playing thirteen-year-old?*

A: *(laughing)*: Not really.

Q: *Would familiarity with computer-game instruction do?*

A: I don't see why not.

Q: *Is it* essential *that this person have experience in software editing?*

A: Not necessarily.

Q: *Why not?*

A: Well, it has more to do with simple good language skills. People need to be able to follow the instructions easily.

Q: *Suppose someone could demonstrate that she had these abilities but had never worked specifically editing instructional materials. Would you consider her?*

A: Perhaps. As long as she was organized, could show me that she could work on her own, and could demonstrate editorial capability, I'd be happy.

Q: *Are there reasonable opportunities for advancement?*

A: Oh, my, yes! Our company's in the children's and adult educational materials business. This job is a natural stepping-stone for someone to move on to a computer design position. That's if they're interested in being trained and can handle the operations I've described. As a matter of fact, the woman who is being replaced was promoted after less than a year as an assistant to one of the designers.

Conclusion

What was left out of this ad was more important than what was put in. Here we have a job that actually requires only a few specific skills. What is wanted is a general knowledge of language and syntax, energy, the willingness to take responsibility, and an ability to put material into a computer neatly and accurately. With ambition, the right person could use this job for a real career boost.

RECYCLING COORDINATOR AD

The recycling coordinator ad attracted our eyes for a number of reasons. First, the salary range was quite broad, indicating that the employer hadn't quite made up its mind about what it wanted. Second, it looked like a fine area for career advancement, because of the growing importance of environmental issues.

We talked with Ms. Grimaldi to get her analysis of the job. Here are some excerpts from our interview.

Q: *How many towns are involved in this program?*
A: There are ten towns in the western section of Ulster County that make up the district. Each of these towns has its own recycling manager, who coordinates the activities of recycling for his or her community.
Q: *These ten managers report to the coordinator?*
A: Yes.
Q: *Does the coordinator dictate a standard set of rules for the western part of the county?*
A: No. The rules are autonomous to the individual towns, and the town managers make their suggestions each month of things that they would like to change, add, or subtract. The basic rules are very similar, but we're interested in responding to innovative ideas as much as possible within the budget.

Q: *If the coordinator doesn't dictate the specific rules, then a detailed knowledge of recycling is not essential?*

A: No, but the person should know the basics. The coordinator should have at least some background in that. College is essential. A degree in environmental studies would be a plus, but not essential. The most important aspects of the job are to be able to educate the public about the need and values of good recycling (using advertising and so on) and, as I said, stay within the budget. Also this person would deal with the state and federal agencies that provide support to our recycling program.

Q: *So, an ability to get along with people plus basic management are more important here than recycling training?*

A: Yes, management skills are very important. Maybe more so than anything.

Q: *Why is there such a wide range in the salary?*

A: It's just that a person with more experience would probably do a better job more quickly than one with less.

Q: *Well, would the new person have any support in learning about the job after they were hired?*

A: Oh, yes. They would spend two to three weeks with the outgoing coordinator, and they would have lots of support from the town managers if they ran into any problems.

Q: *Well, with so much support, do you think a bright, capable, enthusiastic person with good management skills and some recycling background might do as well as someone with years of experience in this particular field?*

A: I guess that's true. I never thought of it that way.

Conclusion

Here you have a job that is actually mistitled. It's called "recycling coordinator," but it really isn't, and in fact, it requires no formal recycling training. What it actually requires is an understanding of, and an ability to promote, a variety of recycling activities, as well as managing ten people who already know their jobs. It's a job with far wider appeal than the ad indicates—someone with a flair for administration, management, and a small background in recycling could probably get the job and hold it successfully.

*   *   *

The purpose of this investigation of job titles and job descriptions is to show you that outside of authentic assembly-line work, most jobs have a high number of variables that are hard to reduce to a small number of words. In fact, it could take a small book to describe most jobs fully and accurately.

WRITE YOUR OWN
□

In the following lines write a classified advertisement that could be used to hire someone for a position that you are seeking. Start with the job title and then provide a 50-word description.

Job Title:_____

Requirements:_____

_____

_____

_____

_____

_____

_____

_____

_____

Now look your ad over. What did you leave out? Are there some things about the job you want that you were too proud to admit? Are some facets too subtle to put in? Did the actual writing of the job requirements make you rethink the work?

Job titles are shorthand labels we pick up through early training. We learned their use as children and it stayed with us. "What do you want to be when you grow up?" someone asks a child. The child answers, "a fire fighter," "a lawyer," "an astronaut," or "a nurse." But these answers are only labels; and as is true for labels, they usually contain very little information about the true work.

Job titles are merely hints of who and what the real needs are in any job. Many people avoid or never bother to find out what the actual needs and demands of their careers are likely to be until long after they have gained the skills to do the job. For instance, at least 75 percent of one freshman law class we queried at Georgetown University had never seen the inside of a law office nor discussed the day-to-day practice of law with a practicing attorney—the working conditions, the problems to be solved, the rewards other than money. Many of the students had made the decision to become lawyers simply because they'd heard about it and it sounded interesting or a relative was a lawyer and they were intrigued by the salary and status, or because of some other vague reason.

The lesson of the want ads and job titles is clear: See them as possibilities, as the clues you can use in your career design and in your search through the hidden job market. Use them as information to gauge the level of activity in a particular field.

4

---□---

THE DOMAIN
OF OPPORTUNITY

In the last chapter you recognized the freeing truth of the proposition that you are not now, nor will you ever be, a mere job title. You may ask if this is true for everyone, and if so, how does one account for the multitude of people and organizations that seem to abide by the doctrine "This is the job and don't ask to change it." The proposition *is* true for all, and we can account for the apparent clash with your reality check.

Yes, there are job titles, and people fill them—or rather, people willingly take them on. Right here is the distinction that makes our point: the difference between filling a slot and taking on a challenge. In the last chapter we observed that the job description or job title is part of the furniture of the job layout, and as such is a mere shadow of the potential for any given individual to be all that he or she can be. In many work environments, we instinctively want to play it safe and follow "the book." Employers seem to want to settle for this as well; sometimes they even insist on it. However, even in the heavily structured production and manufacturing industries, the current recognition is that this "work rules" approach is an older, shallower way to run a business.

In high-performance companies, highly specific job titles are flaking away as fast as weathered paint. They are being replaced with more powerful descriptions: associate, co-worker, team player, strategic administrator, facilitator, quality agent, builder, producer, friend. When things are moving so fast, describing the job in terms of a specific task slows down the thinking.

Even if this isn't happening at your company, it doesn't change the conclusion that for today's career voyager a job is not something to fill, it is something to challenge. And you are a challenger, not a name tag, in the process. It is easy to surrender to the rigidities of the well-structured job, but that kind of approach isn't good for your mental or spiritual health or even very helpful in terms of security or permanence. Job titles get lost long before performers do, and specific job titles become obsolete with every new change in market or technology.

THE TRAINING EXPERT:	We can train laid off steelworkers to be computer operators in new industries.
THE HUMANIST:	No, steelworkers can't be computer operators.
THE TRAINING EXPERT:	You don't know how good our training classes are.
THE HUMANIST:	You can't train a title, you can only train a human. First you've got to take the steelworker out of the person, and then he or she can be trained to use other potential skills in a new way.
THE TRAINING EXPERT:	Point taken.

New jobs are created when a complaint ("This product is junk") becomes a request for action ("How do we get this to work better?"), and then expands into a penetrating look at the underlying conditions of the enterprise ("We need to control quality better").

It is valuable to know how to match your problem-solving skills—specifically those that give you pleasure—to useful career destinations: in the offices, shops, labs, libraries, schools, farms, banks, studios, and restaurants that are home port to your personal psychology.

Let's look at some examples of people who use their problem-solving skills to make their work pleasurable and who get paid for doing what they like to do.

DENNIS CONNOR

□

Problem-solving Skill

"I know how to make people feel young again. I know about nutrition and exercise. If a man or woman does what I tell them to do, they leave looking years younger than when they walked in. It gives me a good feeling looking at this new person whose body I helped revitalize."

Application

"I own and manage a spa and have lectured on well-being at a number of companies and schools. I've written a book. I'll never have trouble doing what I want to do so long as people are still concerned about their health and looks."

SOLOMON SNIDER
□

Problem-solving Skill

"I have a real sense of the mystery of cell life. I would rather work in a well-equipped laboratory than eat. I'd rather discover new genetic connections than almost anything."

Application

"It took me several years to realize that research was my strength and love even if it didn't pay so well. I accepted it, and now I run a lab at NIH. I love it, and it would take a lot of pressure to change. I could change employers for more money, but I'd always find a job back in a lab somewhere."

MITA MIGUEL
□

Problem-solving Skill

"When I met my first Macintosh computer, I felt that I'd just scored the biggest advance in my adult life since I learned to drive. I spent eighty hours in the first week learning its ways, and I then begged, borrowed, or stole every piece of software I could get my disk drives around. We were a match made in Computerland."

Application

"I am a computer consultant to three places. One pays me a retainer of $2,500 per month, another pays by the hour, and the third, a school, I do for free—or, more honestly, for the equipment that they get me at a discount. I go home to my work at night and I don't mind it. I'm in demand for as long as I want, and by keeping myself interested and informed, I can virtually name my own jobs, hours, location, and income."

CECILIA MULRONEY
□

Problem-solving Skill

"I'm a born saleswoman. Even before college I was peddling my photo and cosmetic routes. I know how to deal with people face-to-face, get to know them briefly—anticipate their hesitations and objections. I can show them how my product will help them, and book the sale. I'm a great closer. I believe in myself and in the products that I select to sell. I love the fact that I can be mobile. The transactions are short, and I am really on my own. My biggest enemy is paperwork and I avoid it."

Application

"I'm now a space salesman for a popular video magazine series—and the complexity and size of it fascinates me. I've built my earnings into more than $95,000 in recent years with relative ease. And I'm not married to this industry. I could sell used cars or yachts if need be, and love it still."

ACCOMPLISHMENTS
□

You can uncover your strongest problem-solving skills by analyzing past accomplishments. Think about the work you were most proud of in the last five years. Think about the word *accomplishment*. Doesn't it imply solving a problem in a way that gave you pleasure? It means that, and more. To solve these problems you must have had certain skills. What were they? It's important for you to know how to enumerate them.

It may help to open your thinking if you read what one woman told us about the four accomplishments she was most proud of. Her job was developing package designs for a display firm.

- "I'm divorced. I raised a son and daughter single-handedly and did a great job."
- "I bought an old, run-down barn and turned it into a summer house for me and the kids. I did the whole restoration job myself with the help of the kids and a local handyman. In winter I rent it out and it brings in extra money."
- "I won an award for a new design for a display shipper."
- "I started out seven years ago as a staff assistant in a direct marketing company at $300 per week, and now I make $58,000 per year."

Now, let's analyze the skills beind one of her accomplishments:

Accomplishment: Barn Restoration

- "I'm a pretty good *persuader* when I want to be. I persuaded the bank to give me a mortgage at a time when banks were really holding back. They first thought the barn was too much of a risk. They even thought I was a risk. How could I fix up a barn as a busy, wage-earning single parent? But I convinced them."
- "I'm a natural *handywoman*. I can fix anything."
- "I'm not a licensed electrician but I'm a *learner*. I got a book and learned wiring and plumbing and such."
- "I have an *instinct* for real estate. I knew that I could probably rent the barn in the winter once it was finished. My barn is near a university town, so there are always people looking for places."

YOUR ACCOMPLISHMENTS

Now it's your turn. It may not be easy to make this list. It will require a depth of thought that may challenge you because people tend to underestimate their own worth.

So take some time with this exercise. First breathe deeply to relax. Make a list of four accomplishments you can claim in the last five years that, when all was said and done, made you feel pleased with yourself. The accomplishments need not be earth-shattering. Include accomplishments from your private life as well as from work experience.

1. _____
_____
2. _____
_____
3. _____
_____
4. _____
_____

In the spaces below, list the problem-solving skills you think made each accomplishment possible.

1. Accomplishment _____
_____
_____

Key Problem-solving Skills _____
_____
_____
_____
_____

2. Accomplishment _____
_____
_____

Key Problem-solving Skills _____
_____
_____
_____
_____

3. Accomplishment _____
_____
_____

Key Problem-solving Skills _____
_____
_____
_____
_____

4. Accomplishment _____

_____

_____

Key Problem-solving Skills _____

_____

_____

_____

_____

Most of us have more problem-solving skills than we think we do. Make a list of ten skills that recur most often in relation to your past accomplishments.

Recurring Skills

1. _____
2. _____
3. _____
4. _____
5. _____
6. _____
7. _____
8. _____
9. _____
10. _____

What about any problem-solving skills you have that haven't yet shown up in particular accomplishments? They are nevertheless there for everyday use if you need them. Think about it. Can you rebuild old furniture? Organize work flow? Draft a pretty good sales brochure? Manage a meeting? Use a spread sheet? Speak Spanish? Teach? List both the skills that are first-rate and those that—even though they won't set the world on fire—are good. Don't be shy; give yourself credit for whatever you can do that might be called a problem-solving skill.

Additional Skills

1. _____
   _____

2. _____
   _____

3. _____
   _____

4. _____
   _____

5. _____
   _____

6. _____
   _____

7. _____
   _____

Now go back over the Recurring Skills and the Additional Skills lists, and place an asterisk in front of your top five skills.

SKILL/INTEREST CROSS INDEX
□

Now you know more about your problem-solving skills. What do they tell you? The chart below will help you find out. Along the vertical axis, fill in the top five interests you placed an asterisk in front of on page 53. Along the horizontal axis list the top five problem-solving skills listed under Recurring Skills and Additional Skills. Then place an X in five boxes where an interest intersects with a skill in a way that suggests possible job targets.

Top Interests

Top Problem-solving Skills

1. 2. 3. 4. 5.

1. _____

2. _____

3. _____

4. _____

5. _____

All interests and all skills do not necessarily mesh, but if very few of your interests and skills appear to overlap, then you may not have thought them through. Most often, where you have a genuine interest you also have related skills. And where you have a skill, it has been honed to fulfill an interest (past, present, or future). If there is no overlap for your interests and skills, go back and rethink them.

You may see now that what you are doing is beginning to see a version of yourself that may have been hidden before. A new form for your career life is emerging. It may surprise you and even trouble you because it may not be a form others expect of you, or one that you may have grown to expect of yourself. We urge you to let the form take shape as it will. Do not stifle or amputate it. What you will have when these exercises are completed is a creative plan for a new career design. The finer the thinking, the finer the design.

Wherever a cluster of skills appears in an interest column, it indicates a high potential for your controlling a source of work pleasure. If you find that some of your five interests are not supported by skills, sit back and take a long, sober look at the interest. Ask yourself if this is a real interest—since real interests are usually supported by some problem-solving skills. You may discover that the skill is really there—it just didn't get on your list. If it is an important skill, go ahead and add it now. You may be left with interests that are not supported by identifiable skills—for example, "I like raising money for worthy causes" might be an interest not supported by any type of fund-raising skill or experience. You then have three choices.

1. The interest is "unreal."
2. You may have overlooked some real skills that would relate to the interest. It is possible that while you may not have raised money for anything, you know how to do research and how to write interesting letters. This means you would know how to do research for your worthy cause and how to write persuasive letters to patrons.
3. If, after intensive digging, you still find you have no skill in a particular interest (or only the barest skill), then consider the amount of pleasure you derive from the interest. If it is high, it will compensate you for time spent taking courses, reading texts, going to lectures, and otherwise boning up and developing problem-solving skills in the field.

The next exercise presents a chance to use your personal understanding of the merger of interests and skills. The result may surprise you. Follow the instructions carefully and remember to put in at least as much as you expect to get out. In short, use 100 percent of your imagination and perception for this one.

*JOB POSSIBILITIES I—*FROM SKILLS AND INTERESTS
□

Think about each "intersection" you have checked, and list below some of the job prospects they suggest: where skills and interests combine in possible opportunities.

List ten job possibilities below:

1. _____
2. _____
3. _____
4. _____
5. _____
6. _____
7. _____
8. _____
9. _____
10. _____

If you are not totally satisfied with the selection of job possibilities from this exercise, you can go back and check different "intersections," or go further back and list different skills and interests in the grid. This exercise can give you a full portfolio of career destinations.

JOB POSSIBILITIES II—CURRENT PROBLEMS

Here is a different approach to job possibilities:

1.   Think seriously for a while about today's social, economic, and environmental problems: global, regional or local. On a blank sheet, list as many of these as you possibly can.
2.   Choose three of these that capture your mind and heart as the most interesting. Write them below.

> 1. _____
> 2. _____
> 3. _____

3.   Of these three, now choose the *one* about which you feel you know the most. Write it at the top of the form below. (You can do others by duplicating this form.)
4.   In the first column, list the effects stemming from this problem. List everything from the people impacted to the other problems arising from this.
5.   In the next column, write possible solutions and actions to meet the need.
6.   In the third column, jot down job possibilities which could represent potential for you.

Pick one current social, economic, or environmental problem from your list, and write it below.

Current Problem _____

What are the effects from this problem which need to be attended to?	What are some of the actions and solutions that could help lessen these effects?	What are some job possibilities that would bring the actions and solutions into being?

Repeat form, if you wish, for other situations.

Now recap five or more problem-solving jobs related to the above problem.

1. _____

2. _____

3. _____

4. _____

5. _____

Read these over and be sure that you are putting down more than just job titles. The key to this exercise is that the jobs must solve problems where there are problems to be solved.

Carry the freedom of thought and creativity you've just expressed into the next chapter.

5

DESIGN YOUR
OWN CAREER

In the 1990s and beyond, the number of careers you can discover or invent are endless. The following lists explore jobs that have been created and continue to be upgraded in the dynamic hidden job market.

List ten solid jobs that existed ten years ago and still have a good future—even in an altered or upgraded form.

Our List   **Your List**

1. Bank manager   1. _____
2. Salesperson   2. _____
3. Airline pilot   3. _____
4. Teacher   4. _____
5. Lawyer   5. _____
6. Coach   6. _____
7. Diplomat   7. _____
8. Accountant   8. _____
9. Consumer advocate   9. _____
10. Jeweler   10. _____

Now list ten present jobs that did *not* exist in the mainstream ten years ago.

Our List

1. Personal fitness coach
2. Eurocurrency trader
3. Recycling consultant
4. Biogeneticist
5. Interactive video designer
6. Laser graphics expert
7. Wellness manager
8. Computer resume counselor
9. Video game designer
10. Gray Panthers advocate

Your List

1. _____
2. _____
3. _____
4. _____
5. _____
6. _____
7. _____
8. _____
9. _____
10. _____

The process of creating new work assignments goes on whether the economy is expanding or contracting. With every social, political, and industrial change, old-fashioned, low-value, or obsolete careers get phased out and new problem-solving, opportunity-generating positions arise in the hidden job market. Each of these comes equipped with new titles, duties, and personal challenges.

Invent at least one brand-new career possibility in each field listed below.

Education

_____

Computers

_____

Communications

_____

Human Resource Managing

_____

Transportation

_____

Television

_____

Photography

_____

Food

_____

Energy

_____

Retailing

_____

Ecology and environment

_____

Advertising

_____

Leisure life   Manufacturing

_____   _____

Medicine   Accounting

_____   _____

Optics   Sports

_____   _____

Finance   Crime detection

_____   _____

Electronics   Social care

_____   _____

Even a quick pass at these lists will show you a broad range of fresh opportunities. If you had any trouble with the exercise, we urge you to unleash more of your imagination. Perhaps some quick brainstorming will fire off a new train of thought. Here are some wild ideas to spark your thinking:

□ *Education.* Courses based in modern neuroscience and artificial intelligence that teach people to learn new problem-solving skills. Room here for ways to retrain workers, and nurture the poorly educated in basic skills.

□ *Communication.* A jellylike computer brain that works almost as fast as the human brain but operates on cheap chemical energy and never complains. People to create, build, service, and report about this field.

□ *Transportation.* Immense "low and slow" fuel-efficient aircraft that can carry more than a thousand people and thousands of tons of cargo safely and economically at sonic speeds. Pilots, attendants, mechanics, salespeople.

□ *Photography.* Crystal-clear still and moving photographs on paper, film, video, or computer screen—based on digitized information from computerized hand-held cameras. Producers, directors, technicians, writers, actors, and promoters.

□ *Personal care.* Cosmetic surgery as common as dentistry; new foods with healthful qualities built in; safe acne cures; permanent reversal of eye ailments that greatly reduce the need for corrective lenses. Paramedics to coach, teach, correct, and redirect people with eating, heart, or substance-abuse disorders.

☐ *Leisure life.* New levels of popular sport, including a daring acrobatic version of mountain climbing; electronically enhanced tennis; personal submarines at reasonable cost; night golf; global interactive computer games; advances in music making; new forms of food and cookery.

☐ *Finance.* Money for investment in personal development and education paid back from the higher returns of more productive job-seekers and technology-driven production. New ways to tax and to provide a financial safety net for the troubled or disabled. Financial coaches, electronics funds engineers, wealth creators, and wealth managers.

Innovations and discoveries are constantly developing into job opportunities—with new work relationships. Technological shifts—as well as social, political, and economic ones—are redefining the job market. This means that future society has millions of new problem-solving needs. They will make it possible for all thoughtful and dedicated careerists to find great work pleasure with good job benefits.

Many apparently stable fields have had, and will continue to have, dramatic changes. This wide-angle view of the job world shows how all career designs, including your own or one you may want, are in constant flux; it may also remind you of your own role in the creative process.

Let's take a closer look at what the increase in job opportunities means to you.

DESIGNING FUTURE JOBS I
☐

1. Name the career field you are in now, or one you would consider entering.

   _____

2. In your view, what are the most likely future areas of growth and decline in this field?

   Growth _____

   _____

   Decline _____

   _____

3. What areas within the career field do you think will offer the greatest growth potential?_____

_____

4. What specialized skills or training would you need to keep up with the areas of greatest growth, and how could you get them?

_____

_____

5. List three organizations in this field that you feel are among the most progressive and intelligent in planning for the future.
   a. _____
   b. _____
   c. _____

6. What outside events (technological, social, political, economic, etc.) could most likely have a serious impact on this career field in the next five to ten years?

_____

_____

_____

7. Think up three fresh job situations in this field that could offer growth and personal satisfaction.
   a. _____
   b. _____
   c. _____

Repeat this process for two more career areas on the following forms.

DESIGNING FUTURE JOBS II
□

1. Name the career field you are in now, or one you would consider entering.

_____

2. In your view, what are the most likely future areas of growth and decline in this field?
   Growth_____

   _____

   Decline_____

   _____

3. What areas within the career field do you think will offer the greatest growth potential?_____

_____

4. What specialized skills or training would you need to keep up with the areas of greatest growth, and how could you get them?

_____

_____

5. List three organizations in this field that you feel are among the most progressive and intelligent in planning for the future.

   a. _____

   b. _____

   c. _____

6. What outside events (technological, social, political, economic, etc.) could most likely have a serious impact on this career field in the next five to ten years?_____

_____

_____

7. Think up three fresh job situations in this field that would offer growth and personal satisfaction.

   a. _____

   b. _____

   c. _____

DESIGNING FUTURE JOBS III

1. Name the career field you are in now, or one you would consider entering?

_____

2. In your view, what are the most likely future areas of growth and decline in this field?

Growth_____

_____

Decline_____

_____

3. What areas within the career field do you think will offer the greatest growth potential?_____

_____

_____

4. What specialized skills or training would you need to keep up with the areas of greatest growth, and how could you get them?

    _____

    _____

    _____

5. List three organizations in this field that you feel are among the most progressive and intelligent in planning for the future.

    a. _____

    b. _____

    c. _____

6. What outside events (technological, social, political, economic, etc.) could most likely have a serious impact on this career field in the next five to ten years?_____

    _____

    _____

    _____

7. Think up three fresh job situations in this field that would offer growth and personal satisfaction.

    a. _____

    b. _____

    c. _____

If you gave serious thought to your answers, you should have a good handle on some of the things that can or will happen in several fields within the hidden job market. With the right techniques you will be able to find a personal career target with the correct combination of:

□ The work itself.
□ Where you work.
□ The way you work.
□ Whom you work for or with.

ONE VOYAGE—MANY PORTS
□

Many of the changes in the future job market will simply pop out of the box, unexpected and unpredicted. Career voyagers are well advised to be prepared for several *different* kinds of work and work styles in one lifetime, for not following a predefined career plan. Your skills, talents, and abilities may be sold to the same company, in the same field, or in a new field with entirely different kinds of working situations.

Unfortunately, our culture has encouraged many of us to become specialists or to try to stay with one employer for life. We have been trained in the contexts of scarcity and fear. Our career outlooks have become boxed in. However, the old courtesies of corporate loyalty and fealty are passé. Many people have devoted their futures to companies that then merged, were sold or spun off or otherwise altered by market forces, and then leave their employees out in the cold with obsolescent specialties. Employers can't and don't provide lifetime job security anymore.

Once you become acclimated to the idea of being responsible for your own new career destinations, the future presents refreshing and liberating alternatives. You are not locked in to one career choice unless you choose to do so. Even if you do, the possibilities you may discover may very well change your mind. The success of your career depends on how well you can focus and refocus on your own interests, motivation, and problem-solving skills and on the best thinking and action strategies.

Your work in this chapter can help clear up your thinking about how to penetrate the hidden job market. It will identify opportunities you might not have been aware of or which you might have thought were impossible.

Keep the following points in mind as your proceed on the next stages of your voyage into the hidden job market. Jobs are not static. They change constantly. There are more than 100,000 job changes every day: today, tomorrow, and 260 working days each year. And that is only in this country. And the number is expanding as diversity, technology, and personal career entrepreneurism continue to gain. The job that was closed to you at 3:00 P.M. Monday may be open to you at 9:00 A.M. Friday. Or next Thursday at five. Or ten miles down the road. The job that doesn't exist as you go to bed tonight may be created before you get up for breakfast tomorrow.

6

---□---

WHERE ARE YOU NOW?

Where are you now? What do you know about yourself as a career voyager in the hidden job market that you didn't know when you started this journey?

In answering the following, if any question reminds you of one you've answered before, *do not go back* to see what you wrote. You may have changed your mind since then. The more you learn about yourself, the wider your view of job opportunities will be. Consequently your answers to the same questions may change, as will your expectations.

1. In your present or most recent job, what values are most meaningful to you?

   Work pleasures

   _____   _____

   _____   _____

   Job benefits

   _____   _____

   _____   _____

2. If you could live and work anywhere in the world, where would you choose to be?

   First choice: _____

   Second choice: _____

   Last choice: _____

3. How would you most like to dress in your workplace?
   Day-to-day: _____
   Special events: _____

4. Draw a vertical line to show where you would rate yourself today on an excitement scale from 0 (drudge) to 10 (excited about my work).
   0_____10

5. Rank the following pleasures in order of their relative importance to you.

   _____ Physical pleasures   _____ Interpersonal pleasures
   _____ Sensual pleasures   _____ Communication pleasures
   _____ Intellectual pleasures   _____ Mechanical pleasures
   _____ Creative and aesthetic   _____ Emotional climate
   pleasures   conditions

6. There are 10,000 days in the average person's working career. How many days do you have left? _____

7. If you have worked at the same organization or job area for at least five years, what is the major factor keeping you with this company or job?

   _____

   _____

8. How did you get your present (or most recent) job?
   _____ Sent out letters _____ Advertisement _____ Word of mouth
   _____ Placement   _____ Other methods
   agency

9. Approximately how many full days or equivalent did you spend job hurting before accepting the one you took? _____

10. What is the minimum monthly salary on which you could live? $____

11. What are your two most valuable or marketable problem-solving capabilities?

    _____

    _____

12. What are your three most satisfying interests and what percentage of time do you now spend on them?
    a. _____ _____ percent
    b. _____ _____ percent
    c. _____ _____ percent

13. Assuming you had to make a change, what new growth fields attract you the most?

    _____

    _____

14. If you could switch jobs for two years with someone you know, who would it be? _____
    Why? _____

15. What is the most satisfying job (not considering salary) that you could imagine or invent for yourself? _____
    _____
    _____

7

---□---

JOB FAMILIES

You have already looked at two approaches to uncovering job possibilities—Skill/Interest Cross Index (page 78) and Problem-Solving Jobs (page 81). Here we move into a third important approach to your job targets.

The concept of the job family will provide one of your richest natural resources for penetrating the hidden job market. *A job family* includes dozens of specific jobs and problem-solving opportunities. A job family may be an *industry*—movies, plastics, cosmetics, engines. It may provide a *service,* such as sales, mental health, transportation, travel, or legal. It may refer to an *artistic activity*—painting, performing, graphic design, or writing. It may be in the public interest—counseling, social work, teaching, or crime detection. It could relate to *location or work environment* and deal with forestry, sailing, fishing, or jobs in Amsterdam.

A job family can be any area of personal interest that is broad enough to include a variety of work opportunities. Here's a list of some of the job possibilities under one familiar heading:

Job Family—Automotive

Designing cars	Repairing trucks
Working in car production	Repairing cars
Selling cars	Running a garage
Transporting cars	Running a trucking garage
Driving a cab	Managing a fleet of cabs
Driving a bus	Managing a car company
Driving a racing car	Writing automobile commercials
Designing racing cars	Managing a trucking company
Working in a pit	Teaching driving
Selling tickets to auto races	Writing a book about car repair
Promoting races	Making car parts
Operating a filling station	Selling car parts
Selling tires	Selling antique cars
Operating a fleet of limos	Energy conservation
Writing about antique cars	

The main criterion in selecting a job family is your *interest* in it. It may be an area in which you have a specific proven skill; it may be an area in which you feel you have a chance to grow and learn; or it may be simply a field that you find intriguing but which you don't yet know much about. For example, computerized home office is a relatively new job family. The hidden job market in this job family could hold:

Computer tutor	Business consultant
Training consultant	Financial planner
Software designer	Brochure designer
Software editor	Home office consultant
Hardware sales	. . . and dozens more.

THE JOB FAMILY PROCESS

□

Step 1

Review our list of ninety-three sample job families below. First, cross out all the categories that hold no allure. From the remainder, select four job families that particularly appeal to you, or add a category that interests you even if it's not on the list. The main criterion for selection is your *interest* in a given job family—don't worry about the fact that you may not have any work experience in the field. Indulge yourself. Dream. Be logical *and* illogical. Take a chance. Spotlight your interests, not just your problem-solving skills and talents.

Job Families

Automotive	Religion	Transportation
Education	Botany	Bookkeeping
Television	Biology	Secretarial
Movies	Physics	Selling
Food	Music	Camping
Packaged goods	Mathematics	Insurance
Entertainment	Electronics	Horticulture
Public speaking	Health and wellness	Zoology
Publishing	Nutrition	Fine arts
Textile	Finance	Museum work
Interior decoration	History	Journalism
Agriculture	Banking	Bicycles
Photography	Fashion	Stamp collecting
Fishing	Advertising	Adult education
Accounting	Machinery	Repair services
Office services	Crime detection	Management services
Investments	Metalwork	Sociology
Sports	Government services	Counseling
Building services	Economics	Career services
Personal services	Politics	Rehabilitation
Paper	Magic	Family services
Travel	Toys	Mental health
Physical conditioning	Military	Oceanography
Computers	Weather	Commercial arts
Recreation	Woodworking	Medicine
Construction	Children's services	Interior design
Conservation	Personnel	Industrial design
Ecology	Communications	Architecture
Engines	Boating	Law
Cosmetics	Real estate	Remedial education
Home office	Synthetics	

Others of your own choice:

_____   _____   _____

_____   _____   _____

Step 2

Once you have selected four job families, put each at the top of one of the Job Family Inventory forms on pages 100–103.

Step 3

Under each job family on the Job Family Inventory Forms, list every conceivable job title, occupation, work description, or problem-solving opportunity that you can think of. If you don't know the official name for the position just write down the idea (e.g., "The person in charge of designing the packaging," "The person who selects guests on panel shows," "The people who scout out craft items for new catalogs.").

Remember, you do not have to like or be qualified for any opening on your list. The point is to unleash your imagination. Free association works most successfully when you don't hamper it with mental or emotional traffic signals, fences, and roadblocks. Just write what occurs to you—let one thought lead to another, and see how the list grows.

List a minimum of twenty work activities under each selected job family, but try for more. If you can come up with a very long list from the top of your head, great; but, as a far-seeking career voyager you might like to help yourself with a little research—scour the classified and business sections of your newspaper, read trade journals in the field, ask the help of a counselor, or call anyone you know who already works in the particular job family. You can also find lots of material in any career reference collection; ask a librarian.

Here are five Job Family Inventory forms. The first is a sample list. The next four are for you.

JOB FAMILY INVENTORY FORM

□

Sample

In the spaces below list *every* job title, position, or problem-solving opportunity you can think of or create, whether it is a job or position you would like to have for yourself or not. If specific organizations or information sources occur to you, list them too.)

Job Family: *Health and wellness*

1. Owning a health food store	26.
2. M.D. career	27.
3. Nursing career	28.
4. Medical technician	29.
5. Designing equipment	30.
6. Doing medical research	31.
7. Health insurance consultant	32.
8. Teach exercises to cardiac patients	33.
9. Spa consultant	34.
10. Physical therapist	35.
11. Psychotherapy	36.
12. Holistic health writer	37.
13. Neonatal counselor	38.
14. Aromatherapist	39.
15. Dietician	40.
16. Lecturer on nutrition	41.
17. Elder care specialist	42.
18. Green products consultant	43.
19. Exercise coach	44.
20. Home health care worker	45.
21.	46.
22.	47.
23.	48.
24.	49.
25.	50.

JOB FAMILY INVENTORY FORM

□

In the spaces below list *every* job title, position, or problem-solving opportunity you can think of or create, whether it is a job or position you would like to have for yourself or not.

Job Family _____

1.	26.
2.	27.
3.	28.
4.	29.
5.	30.
6.	31.
7.	32.
8.	33.
9.	34.
10.	35.
11.	36.
12.	37.
13.	38.
14.	39.
15.	40.
16.	41.
17.	42.
18.	43.
19.	44.
20.	45.
21.	46.
22.	47.
23.	48.
24.	49.
25.	50.

JOB FAMILY INVENTORY FORM

□

In the spaces below list *every* job title, position, or problem-solving opportunity you can think of or create, whether it is a job or position you would like to have for yourself or not.

Job Family _____

1.	26.
2.	27.
3.	28.
4.	29.
5.	30.
6.	31.
7.	32.
8.	33.
9.	34.
10.	35.
11.	36.
12.	37.
13.	38.
14.	39.
15.	40.
16.	41.
17.	42.
18.	43.
19.	44.
20.	45.
21.	46.
22.	47.
23.	48.
24.	49.
25.	50.

Job Family _____

1.	26.
2.	27.
3.	28.
4.	29.
5.	30.
6.	31.
7.	32.
8.	33.
9.	34.
10.	35.
11.	36.
12.	37.
13.	38.
14.	39.
15.	40.
16.	41.
17.	42.
18.	43.
19.	44.
20.	45.
21.	46.
22.	47.
23.	48.
24.	49.
25.	50.

Job Family _____

1.	26.
2.	27.
3.	28.
4.	29.
5.	30.
6.	31.
7.	32.
8.	33.
9.	34.
10.	35.
11.	36.
12.	37.
13.	38.
14.	39.
15.	40.
16.	41.
17.	42.
18.	43.
19.	44.
20.	45.
21.	46.
22.	47.
23.	48.
24.	49.
25.	50.

Done? Take one more vital step: Get someone else to go over your lists with you and help you add more ideas. In this and many of the remaining exercises you could use a support system. This system can include your spouse, a close friend, a teacher, a relative—anyone on whom you can rely to challenge and support your thinking. The earlier exercises dealt with personal material, so it was your own insights that were most crucial. Now, as we enter the action stage, it will be useful to air your ideas occasionally with another person who can bring a fresh perspective and may come up with new and productive ideas you may have missed.

Add up the number of combined work ideas you came up with in all four job families. What is the total?_____

If you are like others who have done this work, you probably have 80 to 100 job situations and problem-solving opportunities. If you have closer to 200 items you probably did some research in your job family—looked at trade magazines, went to the library, talked to people in the field. Good— you're getting your money's worth! However, if you had difficulty coming up with a total of even 50 work ideas, you're headed for trouble. Before you slam into the shoals, let's see how you can navigate better.

Emergency Measures

Let Yourself Go.   Maybe you haven't permitted yourself enough latitude in the job families you've been exploring. Go back and look again. Pick new categories. Then project yourself into each job family and try to see how it functions. *Visualize* the environment—the offices or the factories, the house, the restaurant, the airport, the studio, the laboratory, or any of the many places where each job family is located. Remember to list *all* job possibilities, even those you wouldn't want for yourself. Next, think about the people in each job family. What do they look like? Talk to them. What are they doing? Who works for whom?

Go to the Library.   Look up the field in the card file and see what it tells you. Check business directories. Ask the librarians for help. Look up someone who knows the field. If any of your job families are listed in the classified section of the phone book, call a listing. Tell them you're doing a research project (you are) and ask them questions about the field.

Take a Break.   Have a cup of coffee and go for a walk. Take a few hours off to let the ideas incubate. Then come back and put more energy and creativity into this task.

When you have at least 75 job possibilities named among the four Job Family Inventory forms, go on to the next exercise. Keep moving while the trade winds are blowing!

8

----□----

YOUR PERSONAL
JOB TARGET

Congratulations! When you completed the Job Family Inventory forms, you demonstrated a potent power. You employed the kind of career creativity that is crucial for growth and survival in an age of uncertainty and strangeness.

We hope that completing the forms was an open-minded, spontaneous, and unconstrained exercise. If so, you now have shown yourself how to develop a personal resource that no employment agency, headhunter, job counselor, or personnel officer—and no astrologer, palmist, or fortune teller—can give you. And you can do it over and over. Thousands of possibilities lie just over the horizon.

Now armed, you can approach jobs as you would any other decision or research project. You can more coolly evaluate the hidden job market, think about yourself, note your interests and noninterests, and explore and free-associate. You can rest assured that there are several work pictures in which you fit. Next comes the narrowing down process.

Filter 1. Discards

Read the listings in your Job Family Inventory forms with a truly open mind. Review all the ideas, imagining yourself in each job and seeing how you respond to each potential experience. Cross out all those that are outside of your areas of interest or that simply don't turn you on. Leave all the rest.

Filter 2. Satisfiers

Of the items remaining, circle every job-target idea you think would give you more than average satisfaction and pleasure, whether you feel capable of doing the work or not.

Filter 3. Can Do

From all the job targets you've circled, select ten that you feel you could perform well today if given the opportunity. (You may also include those which you could perform well with a bit of training.)

1. _____   6. _____
2. _____   7. _____
3. _____   8. _____
4. _____   9. _____
5. _____   10. _____

Filter 4. Top Five Job Targets

Out of your ten finalists above, select the five you would be willing to make a serious effort to attain now.

1. _____
2. _____
3. _____
4. _____
5. _____

These are your five real job targets for now. They are like five points on a hidden treasure map.

9

---□---

THE TRUTH DETECTOR

Don't Leave Home Without It

Do you remember that we told you that this book has a built-in truth detector system? Let's see if you've been honest with yourself in your work so far.

Compare your five job targets on the last page with the Skill/Interest Cross Index you filled out on page 53.

1. Do all five of your job targets relate to one or more of the interest statements?
   Yes ____No____ If the answer is no, which job targets don't relate?
   _____
   _____
   _____

2. Do all five of your job targets relate to one or more of your problem-solving skills?
   Yes ____No____ If the answer is no, which job targets don't relate?
   _____
   _____
   _____

If any of your job targets do not relate to your interest statements, go back to the Pleasure Profile on pages 58–62 and see if the job target relates to this broader interpretation of your pleasures. If so, it probably is a legitimate target.

Of course, if a job target you've chosen relates to none of your previously listed pleasure indicators, you may have overlooked a hidden interest implicit in the job. This means you may have to add to your list of interests.

However, if your job target does not relate to any of your pleasure indicators, and does not conceal a buried interest, then you need this reminder: One of the key criteria of a job target is that it is personally appealing. Perhaps you selected job targets that seemed more practically attainable in the current job market, rather than selecting those you really would like. This could be shortsighted. Review the entire job family containing that job target, or else go and dig for another job family, and come up with more satisfying work activities. If you settle for less, you'll get less.

In our view, an interest without a skill is a happier state of affairs than a skill without an interest. The former situation could be more profitable, too, even though the latter may seem more practical in a tight job market. The skill without the interest can ensnare your career in morbidity, whereas a high interest can be the motivation for developing skills and finding joyful work.

If your job targets are not connected to either a satisfying pleasure indicator or a problem-solving skill, go back to the beginning and start again. The buzzer just sounded. You've been kidding yourself.

10

---□---

YOUR PERSONAL CAREER MAP

Plotting the Course

In the next chapters you will be able to draw some detailed navigational charts for your career voyage. We will present an integrated, step-by-step program for finding or creating the job target you selected. In order to organize the information that results from this program you will use the Job Action Plan.

Your Job Action Plan helps you plot your campaign; it makes for efficient organization of time in the best interest of your objectives. The two main factors to consider are:

1. A realistic date by which you should, or must, locate a job target you can find suitable.
2. The number of hours you will invest in your job-target campaign each week.

Obviously, if you are unemployed and/or running low on money, you need to put more work and time into reaching your job target and getting a good job. However, remember to work smarter, not harder. (We recommend that you invest no more than twenty to twenty-five hours per week on a job campaign, and that you use the rest of your time for activities that let you unwind, learn, or keep your health and sanity.) If you are still employed and have decided to go after something that will give you more work pleasure as well as a bigger paycheck, a more relaxed campaign of five or six hours each week will be more than enough to handle.

In either case, you should work at prescheduled times.

How long will your job campaign take? There is no single answer to this question. On the average, a well-run campaign (one that gets offers in targeted areas) seems to take between 200 and 500 hours of concentrated effort. A key indicator of a well-run job campaign is that you receive at least three reasonable (and interesting) job offers to choose from.

A good way to start the plan is to determine the date by which you feel you must make the job change. Then, plan backwards from that date.

For instance, assume the exciting new job you finally accept will be selected from at least three job offers. For each offer, you will probably have had four or five interviews. For each interview you obtain, you probably will have to send out ten letters and resumes and make at least fifteen phone calls. It could take an average of one hour of research to find each prospective employer to whom you send a letter and resume. (But figure a little less on the average, because some research will cover more than one such approach.)

Thus, the job you accept will be the result of roughly:

  3 job offers
  15 interviews—exploratory, as well as those for specific jobs
  150 letters and resumes
  225 telephone calls
  100 hours of job market research and networking.

On the following pages are two Job Action Plan forms. These are time schedules—one a weekly breakdown, the second a daily—for you to use as you implement the specific job-campaign actions called for in the coming chapters. (It is a good idea to keep these Job Action Plan schedules, as well as copies of the other forms you will be using, in a three-ring binder.)

To use the Job Action Plan forms, sit down at the beginning of the week and plot what you want to accomplish in that week. List these planned activities on the Weekly Job Action Plan as specifically as you can. Do the same with the Daily Job Action Plan before each day's effort.

At the conclusion of each day and week, note what you have actually accomplished in the period. Compare them with your objectives to make the next daily or weekly Job Action Plan more realistic and effective. You will need many copies of the forms, so prepare them beforehand.

WEEKLY JOB ACTION PLAN

□

You will want to use a separate copy of this form for each job target and for each week. Please make sufficient copies for your campaign.

Week beginning _____   Job Target _____

Major objective for the week _____

_____

_____

General job-market research objectives for the week _____

_____

_____

_____

Time Allocated

General objectives for outside contacts for the week _____

_____

_____

Time Allocated

Additional activities (book exercises, role plays, etc.)_____

_____

_____

_____

Time Allocated

Weekly Time Chart

Activity	Mon.	Tues.	Wed.	Thurs.	Fri.	Sat.	Sun.
	Estimated number of hours to be spent						
Planning							
Self-research							
Job-market research							
Telephone calls							
Letter writing							
Nonjob trips (libraries, interviews, etc.)							
Job interviews							
Meetings with third parties							
Daily total							

Weekly total _____

End of week recap:

What was accomplished?

_____

_____

What objectives were missed?

_____

_____

_____

DAILY JOB ACTION PLAN

Use a separate copy of this form for each job target and for each day.

Date_____   Job Target_____
Job work hours scheduled from _____ *to* _____
*Prime objective for the day*_____

_____

TELEPHONE CALLS, LETTERS, RESUMES

Person/Organization Phone Number & Address	Objective	Result
1.		
2.		
3.		
4.		
5.		

SPECIFIC RESEARCH OBJECTIVES

Sources to Contact	Objective	Result
1.		
2.		
3.		
4.		
5.		

MISCELLANEOUS OBJECTIVES FOR THE DAY

(People to see, places to go, interviews to schedule, etc.)

1.
2.
3.
4.
5.

RESULTS OF DAY'S ACTIVITIES

Accomplishments

Unsatisfied objectives

11

□

SHOALS AND ICEBERGS
Personal and Psychological Dangers

This chapter addresses taking action and relinquishing excuses for not taking action. It examines how old patterns of thinking, inner conversations, habits, beliefs, and entrenched assumptions about ourselves can hinder or help the progress of our search for new employment. We put *hinder* before *help* because now that we have the right information and underlying strategies for the self-directed career voyage, the only thing that can really stop us is the inner workings of our mind-set. Wait, you say. There are a hundred things that can stand in the way: the economy, scores of unreturned calls, the economy, the unemployment rate, the heavy competition, the economy . . . Still we stay with our assertion that it is one's own internal processes that tend to keep one unemployed or underemployed.

The basis for this is our conviction that a well-organized job search is a dependable step-by-step process that, when followed relentlessly, contains the right ingredients for almost anyone to secure life-giving work. However, we know that things don't always turn out that way. The process grinds to a halt. People get discouraged and give up. The momentum slows, the jitters start, and the once bold turn pale. The reasons and imaginings of a world of scarcity and problems overcome the prospects of possibility and abundance. This is natural, but it's also avoidable.

Actually, while the jitters themselves might not be avoidable, the associated personal slowdown is. It is all right to feel discouraged, alone, unwanted, or at a loss for self-esteem. It is not necessary to stop the action plan when this happens. The period when you're worried is the most important time to stay with an action plan. The cost of going off the plan when the going gets rough can be severe. The sights come down, our willingness to accept the next reasonable thing to come along increases, and the tendency to make excuses for lack of success flares up like a rash; we're liable to make an emergency stopover at a job that isn't close to what we really want to do.

This part of the book is about how to continue to take action when your internal mechanisms want to bring things to a stop.

❖ **Rule of the road:** *Stop, look, listen . . . then act.*

ACTIONABLE ITEMS

If you have discovered that your job is about to be eliminated, get busy at once. Use the time you have left to lay the foundation of a well-organized career campaign. Act while still in possession of office facilities and secretarial help. When you are in daily contact with people in your field, be sure to let it be known discreetly that you are actively shopping for something better. Don't infect others with doubt or worry. Keep these emotions to yourself, your family and close friends, or a personal counselor.

Here is a short list of items that are always open for action.

The Written Job Plan

Planning and action are the antidotes to fear and sloth. That's why you should prepare a well-thought-out written plan—including ideas on our forms (pages 118–19) and your own—that should include:

- □ Job targets (perhaps a separate plan for each target).
- □ A time budget (specific hours each day and week to go into your plan).
- □ Weekly quantified goals.
- □ Monthly quantified goals.
- □ An active schedule and calendar on paper, or in a computer or a notebook to keep you apprised at the end of each day and week whether you are falling behind or staying abreast of your goals, and whether your goals are unrealistic and should be revised.

Action Resumes

Your resumes are living documents. Get them current and keep them active.

Action Cover Letters

Take the time to find out as much as possible about the people to whom you are sending your resume. Your cover letters should be appropriately personalized to relate to the specific needs of the companies you select.

Active Research

Read or review a variety of sources of information about possible job opportunities, such as trade journals, business directories, and newsletters. Read books that can point you in productive new directions.

Active Support System

Work actively with your family and trusted friends to brainstorm, give you feedback on your targets and your resume, provide leads and help keep you entertained.

Active Psychological Balance

Twenty to twenty-five hours per week is enough time to spend actively on your job search; five to six hours is adequate if you are currently employed. As tight as things might be, you *must* take time off for other things—play, sports, personal projects, recreation, study, etc. Schedule enriching, rewarding activities to help you keep life in balance. Outside of your "quota" don't complain about or harp on the job search. Share small successes along the way. It is better to be highly focused for a few hours than to spend much more time operating without a plan or strategy.

Practice makes perfect. Once you experience good job-finding approaches that help you get what you want in your life, they are yours for keeps. With the skills to always attain satisfying work, you will have more control of your future, a saner, healthier approach to the often upside-down work world, and more long-term financial security.

BARRIERS AND EXCUSES
□

In the context of a job campaign, a barrier is an internal force that causes immobility at a time when maximum mobility is called for. Barriers are deep and persistent, and they can be part of the general patterns of our behavior. Barriers generally show up in the path of the actions that are necessary in the job search.

An excuse is a justification for not taking an action which could further the outcomes we claim to desire. An inner barrier, such as fear of rejection, will show up in the form of a rationalization or urgent change of plans. For instance, just as we are reaching the part of our plan that calls for us to make some cold calls, the excuses start—I'd like to make these calls now, but it's Friday afternoon and most people have already left for the weekend. I'll do it Monday . . . or next summer . . . or not now in any case.

You've learned by now that this book gives you a lot of work to do. Step, step, step. The pace could seem relentless until you discover that each step is toward the successful realization of something you want. And yet we allow inaction, disguised by excuses, to stand in the way of our best efforts.

To train you to spot these dangerous, self-defeating excuses in yourself or others, let's examine the inaction syndrome.

1. CREATIVE JOB-FINDING ACTIONS
□

The activities below have been used by successful job-seekers. Check off those that you think *could* be useful to your own job campaign.

_____ Spend money on important job aids, such as a course in a job area in which you may discover a fit, or a session with a consultant or counselor.
_____ Make serious plans to turn a pleasurable hobby into a profession.

_____ Think seriously about working in another city, state, or country.

_____ Contact authors of books or articles in your targeted field, or trade publication editors, to see what information they might have that could prove helpful.

_____ Visit the placement office of your old school, even if you haven't been there for ten years.

_____ Thoroughly evaluate your nonwork achievements and translate them into meaningful work-related opportunities.

_____ Call a firm for which you might like to work, although it is not hiring at the present, for a possible interview.

_____ Spend $75 on long-distance calls for job exploration.

_____ Obtain the job sections of out-of-town newspapers.

_____ Use good sales techniques to rewrite your resume and upgrade its sales appeal.

_____ Contact people working in your target field and ask them for advice on what's changing in the field.

_____ Find unlisted jobs by contacting accountants, lawyers, bank officers, friends, former co-workers, relatives who have business connections, etc.

_____ Visit a technical or professional society relating to your field to see if you can get leads and advice.

_____ Ask for honest feedback from anyone you trust.

_____ Order attractive personal letterhead.

_____ Spend three hours studying an organization in which you are interested and with which you are going to have an interview.

_____ Call up two or three successful friends and ask for a few minutes of problem-solving advice.

_____ Ask for a transfer if you are dissatisfied with your job.

_____ Quit your job now.

_____ If you are currently unemployed, set up a buddy system with other unemployed persons to help one another in your job campaigns.

_____ Obtain the creative partnership of your spouse or close friend on a daily basis for helping you solve job-action problems.

_____ Take a couple of days off from your present job—either on sick leave or vacation—in order to explore other kinds of work.

_____ Get an interview in a field you instinctively might not consider seriously that could possibly give considerable work satisfaction once you got to know it.

2. THE EXCUSES

□

Of the creative job-finding actions you've checked, select three that could give you a boost in your own campaign.

List one of these on each of the forms on pages 121–22. Under the column marked Excuse, write down all the reasons a typical job-seeker or you yourself might find to avoid taking these actions. Even if you are not considering taking this job action now, dream up the excuses that might be used.

To show what we mean, here is a sample from the job-action list of a man who attended one of our workshops—Harry Roman, a stockbroker from Phoenix who was interested in getting into horse ranching.

Creative Job Action *Contact editors of trade publications in a job-target field and interview them, in person or by phone, for advice.*

Excuse	Actions to Overcome Excuse
1. *I don't know what the journals are.*	
2. *The editors are probably very busy. Why would they talk to me?*	
3. *What advice could they give me that I don't already know?*	
4. *I couldn't make these calls from work.*	
5. *I'd never get past the executive assistant.*	

Now it's your turn.

Creative Job Action_____

_____

_____

_____

Excuse	Actions to Overcome Excuse

Creative Job Action_____

_____

_____

_____

Excuse	Actions to Overcome Excuse

_____
_____
_____
_____
_____
_____
_____
_____

Creative Job Action_____

_____

_____

_____

Excuse	Actions to Overcome Excuse

3. OVERCOMING EXCUSES

□

We'd like you to look over the Excuse columns in the three forms you filled out. In the space provided on the right, come up with a remedy or action that should answer or overcome each excuse. Be a problem solver. If you find some of the excuses difficult to overcome, call in your support system and see what they might come up with. Before you do this, you might also want to take a look at the remedies Harry Roman thought of.

Creative Job Action *Contact editors of trade publications in a job-target field and interview them, in person or by phone, for advice.*

Excuse	Actions to Overcome Excuse
1. *I don't know what the journals are.*	1. *Call someone in the field and ask; stop in at the library.*
2. *The editors are probably very busy. Why would they talk with me?*	2. *How do I know they are too busy? Just invent myself a research project or survey. I need only 15 minutes or so.*
3. *What advice could they give me that I don't already know?*	3. *They could give me leads to job titles, books, association people.*
4. *I couldn't make these calls from work.*	4. *Take a day off. Take two.*
5. *I'd never get past the executive assistant.*	5. *Tell him that I'm working on an important project and was told that his boss was the best person to help.*

Making excuses is a normal part of a job search. It's how you overcome excuses that determines your eventual success on your career voyage. You will notice, however, that the more accurately you identify your job target, the less likely you are to make excuses for not finding it.

From here on, you will be presented with ideas, strategies, and approaches that have proven successful and that when properly used, are virtually guaranteed to get you a satisfying job suited to your real skills and talents.

12

---□---

THE HIDDEN
JOB MARKET

The hidden job market is that vast reservoir of job information that people in companies, associations, and other organizations have about changes and developments in their own work environments. Even though any one individual has only a few pieces of the mosaic, the accumulation of bits of information contributes to a complete picture.

The hidden job market includes people's knowledge of unreleased new product plans, emerging cost problems, impending retirements, and the expansions and contractions within a particular department or company or in an entire industry. This realm includes the jobs that may (or may not) be advertised in a few weeks; last week's advertised jobs that haven't yet been filled; the jobs that were quietly released to only one or two agencies; and the openings that are being posted internally or via an old-boys' network first.

In addition, the pressures of the marketplace force organizations to change direction constantly—new products, new strategies, new work force. Every time a change is made, some jobs open, some jobs shift, some close.

This hidden job market—the whole realm of interactions lying just below the surface—is generally unseen by the average job-seeker. You have a distinct advantage over others as a career voyager—you know how to explore this realm and discover possibilities before they do.

By knowing how to make the most of the hidden job market, you can open up new avenues in your thinking. You can venture beyond normal career horizons, assured that innumerable possibilities are available to choose from. However, this demands persistence on your part.

Of course, there are no job postings in the hidden job market; this is not an area organized into neat headings and columns. Instead, it exists as a constant swirl of innuendo and projection. Someone might tell you: "Did you hear that Jan's boss is being sent to open up a new branch in Albuquerque? Lucky guy!" This can lead to your finding out what kind of staff is needed in the new location and if the company is expanding in other areas. You could follow this up by getting an introduction to Jan's boss and doing some casual but pinpointed snooping.

You undoubtedly already know that in corporate job handling, many weeks or months can pass between the time the need for a new position is recognized and the time that the personnel department is asked to run an ad or contact employment agencies. Personnel may not even know of the opening at first—line managers may try to get their own leads or ideas in place before "going public" with a job requisition.

Your knowledge of, and commitment to, exploring the hidden job market can keep you months ahead of the competition in ferreting out jobs that are not yet defined.

JOB-MARKET RESEARCH
□

Job-market research is an indispensable activity in exploiting the hidden job market. This is good news and bad news—good because it gives you an important tool, and bad because this kind of research takes time, persistence, and discipline. It also doesn't yield immediate results, and most of us looking (or being forced to look) at a new career direction thirst for immediate results. Once you commit to doing the necessary research, you gain freedom from the bureaucracy that governs traditional job-search methods. It adds up to taking control of the process instead of sitting in waiting rooms and being on waiting lists, hoping for somebody else to take the next step.

Job market research is done in libraries, on telephones, over lunches, during bank hours, and at the breakfast table. The process has three stages. Each involves doing some hard work, but the rewards are worth it.

1. SOURCING

Sourcing refers to selecting *sources of information* to help you translate your job targets into tangible possibilities. Sources of information include business directories, trade magazines, general newspapers, magazines, and the yellow pages. A major source of leads is news media. Look for relevant news on economics, products, people, trends. The sourcing phase includes information about or from other people—second, third, and fourth parties who might know something to help you.

Of course, we don't know what your own job targets are. Consequently, the examples that follow are general ones. You will fill in your Sourcing Inventory forms on pages 135–142 with references to sources of information on your personal job targets.

General Reading

Here are a variety of general sources where you can find references to names and addresses of potential employers that might lead you to your job target.

- Your local newspaper. Current and back issues. News articles, economic news, news relating to your field of interest, product news.
- Out-of-town newspapers. Current and back issues.
- *The Wall Street Journal* and *The New York Times*. Both are international in scope. Current and back issues.
- Classified telephone directories (yellow pages). Both local and those of other locations that interest you.
- General magazines. For product ads and relevant articles.
- Books on your subject of job-target interest.
- College alumni journals. See who is where now.
- Association newspapers or magazines. For news of people and ideas.
- Newsletters in your field of interest.
- Computer bulletin boards and specialized data network connections.

Here are some tips for using general reading sources.

- When reading association newspapers and journals, keep your eyes open for conventions and trade meetings of interest.

□ The back issues of newspapers and magazines are a great source because, surprisingly, classified ads from five or twelve months ago can often be more useful than those that appear today. You may find a company that months ago was hiring for your kind of job target; then it shifted its budgets, but now it could go back in the original direction. It's a lead. What other openings do they have? And what about the old jobs that were filled—did the new hire work out? If so, find out his or her name and call. Here's a knowledgeable colleague, one recently hired in your field of interest. If you approach this person properly you might get some useful suggestions as to where to go—potential openings in related fields or particularly helpful employment agencies.

□ Be on the lookout for news about company relocations. Whom did they lose? What do they now need?

□ If you are thinking of relocating, call your local telephone company and ask for copies of the classified pages for the specific cities or region you'd like to consider. If you don't need the entire directory from each city, you can review copies at the local library and photocopy the sections you want. One job-seeker we knew acquired twenty different directories. Since his target field was furniture design, he canvased dozens of companies listed under "Furniture" in the yellow pages of the cities he chose. He called the companies, persisted in getting through to someone who could answer his questions, and then sent resumes and targeted letters. Eventually he wound up with a job he liked in a city he liked—and a sizable telephone bill that he was delighted to pay.

Directories

There are literally thousands of highly focused directories listing people, companies, products, and publications in almost every possible field of interest. These range from people directories such as *Who's Who* to major business directories published by Dun & Bradstreet, Standard and Poor, and Thomas Register. In addition, virtually every local chamber of commerce publishes a directory.

Once you have decided on a job target, it is a relatively simple matter to locate one or more directories that can lead you to employers in this field. If you don't know which specific directory relates to your job target, ask people in the field to recommend one. It may take several calls, but it is well worth the effort. Most directories can be found in the economic or business section of your local public library, at a business school's libraries, at brokerage firms, and in the offices of your local chamber of commerce.

Superdirectories are directories of directories. They will not give you the names of employers in your field, but they will point you to more specific directories appropriate to your search. Among the most valuable superdirectories are *The Guide to American Directories,* which lists thousands of directories in almost all categories; the *Encyclopedia of Associations,* which contains the names, telephone numbers, and addresses of thousands of different kinds of trade and professional associations (including the one that can put you in touch with employers in your job-target area); and *Standard Rate and Data,* which lists all business periodicals published, by topic.

Your local librarian is your best ally when it comes to locating directories or superdirectories.

A REAL-LIFE EXAMPLE

Allison Cramer would like to handle public relations for an art museum or gallery. When we asked her to name a directory that might be useful, she couldn't think of one offhand. Then she made a telephone call to a friend who makes acquisitions for a local art museum and came back with the title *Who's Who in American Art.* This was a big beginning to getting on the inside track.

What about you?

Get the name of one or more directories containing the names of organizations, associations, companies, corporations, etc., that might have a place for you. Write your answers in below.

Job target _____
    Directory_____
    Directory_____
    Directory_____

Are you still having trouble? Can you think of someone in the field? Pick up the telephone and call her. Ask what directories are most useful. You don't know anyone in the field? Think of a friend you have who might know. Call him. This is how you crack the hidden job market—by taking the time to make contact with others and asking the right questions. And don't worry. If worse comes to worst you can always use *The Guide to American Directories.* That has everything.

Trade and Business Publications

Every business, profession, and endeavor from programming to metallurgy has its own publications. Some are published weekly or monthly, others quarterly or annually. They report ongoing events and trends in the particular field as well as provide extensive information about organizations and individuals in the field. Some of these publications even include help wanted ads.

There probably are many publications in your field of interest. You may already subscribe to some. Go to the library and look up others in *Standard Rate and Data,* a superdirectory. Go through back issues of trade publications and note those employers who interest you. It's worth knowing who was hiring in the area of your job target in the recent past—perhaps they have other similar openings. The articles provide a lot of information about what's going on in the field. They also inform you of the most current jargon. (By the way, be absolutely sure you know what the jargon means before you use any of it. There's nothing that sounds sillier than the inappropriate use of a technical word in an effort to seem smarter than you are. It's much better to stick to common English in your discussions.)

Check for references to books, reports, and individuals related to your job field. Take down the names of the people who wrote articles you found particularly interesting; call them (their company affiliations are often given in the editor's note).

While going through any publication, watch for product advertisements. If any of the products relate to your job targets, it is important to add these companies to your Employer Target List (see page 145).

Name one trade publication in the field of your job target:

_____

Financial Reports and Analyses

If a company is publicly held, annual reports and investment analyses are yours for the asking from brokerage houses. You can find out what the company is doing and what its prospects are. In addition, through their in-house publications, brokerage houses often explore trends in your field.

Government Reports

Federal, state, and local governments prepare reports and studies on almost every activity—both commercial and noncommercial. For material published by the federal government, contact the Government Printing Office. However, if you know, for example, that information that applies to your job target would be in the Department of Health and Human Resources or with the Environmental Protection Agency, contact them directly and ask for a list of their publications.

Third Parties

A third party is anyone who could suggest information that will help uncover the names of organizations or people in your target field. Pulled together, a list of these is your "network." Third party also refers to any organization that might offer information that would lead you closer to, or bring you into contact with, a job target. It's the old who-you-know game. This category includes:

- Relatives, from your immediate family to distant cousins and even ex-mates, and past in-laws.
- Old professors, teachers, and school friends.
- Professionals—lawyers, accountants, your banker, your real estate broker, stockbroker, doctor, consultants, elected officials.
- Fellow employees or a boss from a previous job. Have a lunch or coffee or a telephone chat with one of them, who may know something or someone you should follow up with.
- Editors or writers of articles in trade journals or trade publications, newspapers, or newsletters in your field.
- Big-name authorities. Someone you know may know someone who knows them.
- Helpful organizations—consider college placement offices, trade association executives, officers of the chamber of commerce, and other community contacts. With these groups of people, you can be quite direct in your approach. It's their business to have ideas about job location.
- Priests, rabbis, ministers, insurance agents, local merchants, and suppliers. Your creditors may be valuable contacts because they want you to have a job too!

By now you will have a pretty good idea of how vital *sourcing* is to good research. You should have as long a list of specific potential sources of information relating to your job target as you can possibly think of, imagine, free-associate, guess at. Go as far as your creativity and energy will let you.

It is important that this list of sources be well organized. Look at the sample Sourcing Inventory Form below to see how one job-seeker did this; she had a year's experience and was looking for a better-than-entry-level job. After studying the sample form, use the blanks on pages 135–42 (one form for each job-target area).

SOURCING INVENTORY FORM
□

Job Target *Photographer*

General Reading Sources

List the names of general publications you could screen for potential leads. Include newspapers, books, etc.

1. *Sunday NY TIMES and WASHINGTON POST—photo credits*

2. *Check back issues of above*

3. *Popular Photography*

4. *Camera 35*

5. *Modern Photography*

6. *Better Homes and Gardens (get names of photographers)*

7. *Time-Life photo specials*

8. *Leaders Magazine: Ask for names of good portrait photographers*

9. *The series of books: A Day in the Life of*

10.

Directories and Business Publication Sources

Research and list the names of specific directories and business publications that relate especially to this job target.

1. *Yellow pages under "photographers"*
2. *Midwest Camera Club—membership directory*
3. *Standard Rate and Data (look for publications under photography)*
4. *Editor and Publisher*
5. *Industrial Photography*
6. *Directory of Professional Photography*
7. *Freelance Photographer's Handbook*
8. *ASMP publications*
9.
10.

Financial Institutions and Government Sources

Check for federal, state, or local government listings of organizations or services related to your job target. Seek out information from financial services and reports.

1. *Look up photography in The Dictionary of Occupational Titles*
2. *Get annual reports of Kodak, Polaroid, and Xerox*
3.
4.
5.

Third Party Networks

List anyone who might be able to suggest information leading to the names of organizations, people, or agencies that could move you closer to your job target. If you have more names than the space allows, use extra sheets and attach them to the form.

        Name   Telephone

1. *Phil at the Kodak Information Center* _____
2. *Manager of Westside Photo* _____
3. *Advertising agency contact* _____
4. *Photography editor of Life* _____
5. *Photo instructor from high school (call school for name)* _____
6. *Photographers' association local head* _____
7. *Uncle Harry (works for big printing company)* _____
8. *Helen from the design studio down the block* _____
9. _____
10. _____
11. _____
12. _____
13. _____
14. _____
15. _____

Miscellaneous Sources

List here any other sources you could use to obtain information or contacts.

1. _____
2. _____
3. _____
4. _____
5. _____

SOURCING INVENTORY FORM

Job Target _____

General Reading Sources

List the names of general publications you could screen for potential leads. Include newspapers, books, etc.

1. _____
2. _____
3. _____
4. _____
5. _____
6. _____
7. _____
8. _____
9. _____
10. _____

Directories and Business Publication Sources

Research and list the names of specific directories and business publications that relate especially to this job target.

1. _____
2. _____
3. _____
4. _____
5. _____
6. _____
7. _____
8. _____
9. _____
10. _____

Financial Institutions and Government Sources

Check for federal, state, or local government listings of organizations or services related to your job target. Seek out information from financial services and reports.

1. _____
2. _____
3. _____
4. _____
5. _____

Third Party Networks

List anyone who might be able to suggest information leading to the names of organizations, people, or agencies that could move you closer to your job target. If you have more names than the space allows, use extra sheets and attach them to the form.

Name   Telephone

1. _____
2. _____
3. _____
4. _____
5. _____
6. _____
7. _____
8. _____
9. _____
10. _____
11. _____
12. _____
13. _____
14. _____
15. _____

Miscellaneous Sources

List here any other sources you use to obtain information or contacts.

1. _____
2. _____
3. _____
4. _____
5. _____

SOURCING INVENTORY FORM

Job Target _____

General Reading Sources

List the names of general publications you could screen for potential leads. Include newspapers, books, etc.

1. _____
2. _____
3. _____
4. _____
5. _____
6. _____
7. _____
8. _____
9. _____
10. _____

Directories and Business Publication Sources

Research and list the names of specific directories and business publications that relate especially to this job target.

1. _____
2. _____
3. _____
4. _____
5. _____
6. _____
7. _____
8. _____
9. _____
10. _____

Financial Institutions and Government Sources

Check for federal, state, or local government listings of organizations or services related to your job target. Seek out information from financial services and reports.

1. _____
2. _____
3. _____
4. _____
5. _____

Third Party Networks

List anyone who might be able to suggest information leading to the names of organizations, people, or agencies that could move you closer to your job target. If you have more names than the space allows, use extra sheets and attach them to the form.

Name   Telephone

1. _____
2. _____
3. _____
4. _____
5. _____
6. _____
7. _____
8. _____
9. _____
10. _____
11. _____
12. _____
13. _____
14. _____
15. _____

Miscellaneous Sources

List here any other sources you use to obtain information or contacts.

1. _____
2. _____
3. _____
4. _____
5. _____

SOURCING INVENTORY FORM
□

Job Target _____

General Reading Sources

List the names of general publications you could screen for potential leads.
Include newspapers, books, etc.

1. _____
2. _____
3. _____
4. _____
5. _____
6. _____
7. _____
8. _____
9. _____
10. _____

Directories and Business Publication Sources

Research and list the names of specific directories and business publications
that relate especially to this job target.

1. _____
2. _____
3. _____
4. _____
5. _____
6. _____
7. _____
8. _____
9. _____
10. _____

Financial Institutions and Government Sources

Check for federal, state, or local government listings of organizations or services related to your job target. Seek out information from financial services and reports.

1. _____
2. _____
3. _____
4. _____
5. _____

Third Party Networks

List anyone who might be able to suggest information leading to the names of organizations, people, or agencies that could move you closer to your job target. If you have more names than the space allows, use extra sheets and attach them to the form.

Name   Telephone

1. _____
2. _____
3. _____
4. _____
5. _____
6. _____
7. _____
8. _____
9. _____
10. _____
11. _____
12. _____
13. _____
14. _____
15. _____

Miscellaneous Sources

List here any other sources you use to obtain information or contacts.

1. _____   4. _____
2. _____   5. _____
3. _____   6. _____

2. DIGGING AND SORTING
□

In the next steps we have laid out a systematic approach to ferreting out employer leads. We recommend you use a step-by-step approach because we have seen how results improve when people follow a disciplined system.

At this point in your campaign for mastery of the hidden job market you have located your sources of information and want to use this source material to get the names of particular employers who might have positions relating to your job targets. *Digging and sorting* is investigating the selected sources, extracting information and leads including the names, addresses, and phone numbers of key contacts at potential employers. It also includes discovering other relevant information such as the size of the company, its growth potential, and the name of the head of the department you're interested in. This data can help you make contact with that employer.

First, review all the sources on your Sourcing Inventory forms. Put an asterisk alongside the ten to fifteen publications, people, and organizations that you feel will be the most fruitful sources of potential employer names and contacts. Make at least five copies of the Job Research Form on page 143. Next, select five of your primary sources and list them at the head of a copy of the form. (We recommend you work with no more than five of these forms at a time—enough to keep your research going, and not so many that you are overwhelmed with paperwork.)

Get in touch with each of these first sources; buy or borrow the publication and get the research done: read, phone, scan, burrow, and dig into each source for the names of potential employers. For example, if your job target is computer networking media, one of your sources is probably *Online Magazine*, a popular magazine in the telecomputing field. You would look at several issues, and under the column headed Potential Employers, list all the companies you find advertised or mentioned in articles or announcements that seem worth considering for future contacts or interviews.

JOB RESEARCH FORM

□

[Make at least five copies of this form]

Select one of your most likely sources of information from the Sourcing Inventory forms you filled out. Consult the source, and list all the employer leads you can obtain from it. Then rate the employers (A is best) according to which you think has the best potential for you.

Job Target _____

Information Source _____

To be Found At _____

| Rating for Potential | | | Contact Information: Organization, | Useful Information |
A	B	C	Address, Phone	

When all your employer leads from these primary sources are listed on the five forms you fill out and rate, transfer the information on the fifteen to twenty most realistic and immediate possibilities to the Employer Target List on page 145. Because space is limited on the form we provided, you may want to prepare duplicates, adding extra sheets as needed (or, if you prefer, make up your own format).

While this is a research exercise and not the main game, keep in mind that without the basic research your actions will not be first-rate. Be careful of moving too fast and without the right backup. Action without direction is like a stone thrown into the air, and direction without action is like a fixed road sign going nowhere.

EMPLOYER TARGET LIST

□

Select your most viable prospects from Job Research Forms and list them here. You may need additional copies of this form.

Rank	Employer Target Organization, Address	Name, Title, Phone of Person to Contact	Results and Comment

3. IDENTIFYING THE POSSIBLE AND REAL OPENINGS

□

Identification is the final stage of your research. You have obtained the names of employers who might relate to your job target. Now, it's time to probe these potential employers (by methods we will describe later), to determine whether they currently employ or may need those with the kinds of skills or qualities that are related to your job target. If there is a need you can fill, identify the person in the organization who would be most likely to make the hiring decision for your job target. Starting with the first organization on your Employer Target List, make initial contact with each organization in order to answer two key questions.

1. Are they doing work in any area that coincides with your job target? (Try not to reveal that you are just job searching.)
2. If so, *who* is the person to contact in order to find out more of what is going on in the field?

Note: You do not need to contact this potentially very important person just yet. You simply want to know who he or she is. If you come up negative on either question delete the employer target from the list.

You will undoubtedly be influenced in your selection by geographic location, size of company, style of product it manufactures, reputation, etc. For those who are not eliminated, make comments as appropriate. As you eliminate some names, go back to your Job Research Forms and find new ones. Continue this process of subtracting and adding until you are left with at least fifteen organizations that offer real possibilities for future contact.

Identification Tips

Ask the switchboard operator for the name of the person with the job title to whom you think you might report if you attained your job target.

If the operator doesn't know and switches you to personnel, ask for the name again. If they want to know why you want to know, invent a reasonable, nonthreatening business reason—e.g., you're taking an opinion survey on some subject in the field.

If personnel can't figure out exactly to whom you should talk (because there is no such job or because it has a different title), try calling a senior vice president in your area of interest. If your conversation with him or her reveals that the company has no job title related to your job target, it might be a signal that they need someone like you. If you handle the situation properly, you may be able to create an opening for yourself.

You should also call the editors of trade journals in your field, and ask them what they know about the employer you're interested in, and who would be the person to call.

The process of probing and identifying is a continuing one, and as you go along, you will be constantly revising your Employer Target List. For example, if you find on your first go-around that some of the employers you selected turn out to be nonproductive, don't despair. Go back one or two steps and dig for more names. Or try news sources. Using a variety of sources from your research is an important key to the mystery of the hidden job market.

Remember, just as you researched this one job target, you can research others. The techniques are the same, it is sources of information that differ.

Nothing succeeds like persistence. Sooner or later we believe you will have at least three job targets, each with Employer Target Lists. There will probably be ten to fifteen names on each list. And you will know exactly who you want to reach in all thirty to forty-five companies. How do you reach them? The next chapter, "Getting Inside," will tell you.

13

GETTING INSIDE

We move now from the world of research and preparation to the world of connections. Up until now it has been possible to defer, delay, or question the relevancy of the material and the various assignments and to keep to yourself. Now the exploration of the hidden job market enters the world of face-to-face contacts. In terms of the career voyage, we are approaching at a once distant port and we want to find out if the natives are friendly. Here is where your good navigation pays off.

GOING FOR INTERVIEWS

No matter how good your job targets, research, credentials and resume, or how powerful your network, all job quests arrive at the interview stage, and you will not get an offer unless you have been interviewed. As a matter of fact, you will not score high in the quality of your career options unless you generate many interviews. Just as most businesses won't succeed unless there is a constant stream of sales attention, presentations, meetings, and negotiations, the quality of your career choices is reduced unless you are able to keep connections going with live prospects and to do this without undue anguish.

This chapter describes the strategies for getting you dozens of interviews.

THE TURNDOWN TURNOFF

Here is where the trip can get choppy. Even a warm approach to an unknown yet potential employer carries with it a frightening cargo of disappointment. Calls to arrange for an interview are fraught with rejection and disappointment. A really good job search goes something like: No, No, No, No, No, No, No, No, No, No, No, No, *Yes!* That is the nature of the process for the biggest talents and lesser mortals alike. The thing to do is to get through the no's faster!

While it is easy to see these no's as personal rejections, they are not—they are an inherent part of the process. By directing your energy to the job targets you have selected and contacting employers who may not have announced that they are expecting an opening, you will often find that your timing is off: the need has still not surfaced or perhaps the job was filled a week ago. Even though you are coming in uninvited, you stand a good chance of scoring in the long run with that employer who has just the work you are looking for, in the location you want, at a great salary, and with little or no competition—especially since the job may not have been advertised or announced at the time you get there.

In many cases our very interaction will create the opening. This is the essential nature of mastering the hidden job market: to uncover opportunity for new work situations and not to be dependent on the public marketplace for your connections.

You probably will have to make ten to fifteen phone calls for each interview you get. The pessimist in you complains, What a waste of time—fourteen calls. The optimist says, You know, with an effort, I bet I can have two or three new interviews each week. What's forty calls? Take your pick. At every stage of your job plan you will be doing many things without immediate return. Follow the instructions, put in the time, the effort, the energy, and the answer will be *Yes.*

THE ABCS

An effective approach for getting interviews, the ABCs are:

- *A for Attention.* You must be noticed. They must read your cover letter or they won't read your resume. They must listen to your phone call or you won't be invited in.

□ *B for Benefits.* You must have something to offer—a capability, a problem you can solve, a service you can render, an answer to give. You must also communicate this benefit in sufficiently convincing manner so that the reader or the listener will want to hear more about you and how you can help. Remember the previously mentioned universal hiring rule: Any employer will hire (or interview) any individual if the employer is convinced that it will bring more value than it costs.

□ *C for Closing.* Get the interview scheduled then and there. Ask for and get a specific time commitment—or a definite turndown. It's important to avoid procrastination.

Attention by Phone

The telephone is the most potent job-finding tool you have. In a matter of minutes, you can get in touch with virtually anyone in almost any sphere of activity that interests you.

Once you have contact information, call your targeted organization or person immediately. Even at top levels, many executives answer their own phones, especially before 9:00 A.M. or after 5:00 P.M. So if you get your person's direct number (ask the switchboard), you may get through immediately, or will find out when they will be free and call back later. If neither happens, you still may get to speak to the secretary or someone else in the company who can help you target the timing of your next call. What are you calling about? You have to establish a specific purpose to the call—obviously not that you are looking for work. For example, you want to discuss something about a new contract, a reorganization, a new product, a new direction in the field, etc. Make some notes about the things you want to say, once you do get through, to give the person a good reason why he or she could want to see you. Relate to something of interest to this person or their organization or information you have read or found from your contacts.

Good phone techniques can help you unearth a variety of valuable, exclusive job data. They can help carry your message to almost any ear in the kingdom of work. The positive message you give out about yourself can open doors and minds. It can perform these wonders only if you are willing to express it. (Read Richard Zarro's book on transformed telecommunications, *The Phone Book*).

Phone fright is commonplace. We give up so much personal power to possible rejection that we miss one of our greatest assets. The antidote to phone fear is the knowledge that we can call a virtually unlimited number of people to help us. Keep dialing. Prepare lots of numbers in advance and dial, dial, dial.

PRACTICE EXERCISE

You can overcome your phone fright with a little practice. Start now, grab a phone book, and make ten telephone calls about anything at all—but make the calls to complete strangers who are in businesses or services listed in the directory. Reach someone. Find out about their business. If it makes it easier for you, use a pseudonym. The calls need not relate to an actual work situation and do not have to produce results. Just make them for practice. Here are some examples of the kinds of things you can call about:

- Call your local newspaper and ask to speak to the business editor. Ask him or her how to find out what's going on in a particular area.
- Call a local utility company and ask to speak to the vice president in charge of research. Ask him or her what they are doing in the area of solar energy.
- Call a local department store and speak to the person who would be interested in introducing a new product line.
- Call the mayor's office and inquire about what is being done to provide job counseling to the unemployed.
- Call the sales manager of a manufacturing concern. Say you are doing a research project and want to know to which trade association the company belongs. Then ask for the names of some other organizations in the field.

In this practice, what you say is not that important. Work on sounding confident and relaxed, even though you are talking to people important to you. You will find that many so-called experts or authority figures are willing and pleased to talk with and listen to you. So go ahead. Make ten calls now.

A very important aspect of job-related telephoning, whether you are digging for information or trying to set up an interview, is to organize yourself beforehand.

- Before you make your first call, always be prepared with the names, phone numbers, and information desired for a group of calls.

□ Be ready with a fast, interesting statement that immediately describes a specific benefit for the person with whom you are talking. Saying something concrete will hold their attention.

□ If you don't wish to talk with a secretary who intercepts your call, hang up and try again—early in the morning, during lunch, or after normal work hours. If you decide to stay on the line, be friendly and upbeat. If the secretary asks, "What is this in reference to?" use the same opening as you would with the boss. If it's something the boss would pay attention to, so may the secretary.

□ Breathe slowly, relax, and allow your confidence to be there. Practice. Make lots of calls—both for practice and for real. If possible, record your presentation and analyze it. Eventually, if you are a full-time job seeker, you should spend at least eight hours a week on the telephone, dividing your time between gathering job information, making contacts, and setting up interviews.

Attention via Third Parties

Just as in the research phase, a forceful way of bringing yourself to the attention of people you want to see is through the help of third parties who might have authority or standing in your target field or who have a connection with the organization you are trying to infiltrate. Your third party could be:

□ Someone in the organization.
□ Someone in a professional society.
□ Someone in a trade organization.
□ A trade journal editor.
□ Someone in your local chamber of commerce.
□ Someone in your alumni association who is in the same field.
□ A mutual friend.
□ A college professor.
□ A former boss or an officer at your previous employer.
□ A management consultant or placement counselor in the field.
□ A recognized expert in the field.
□ An important supplier of your target employer.
□ An important client of your target employer.

A third party can help you in several ways. Before a meeting, the third party can find out about particular aspects of the organization or field. If you are clear and convincing in your presentation, he or she might set up an immediate interview, dispensing with the formality of your sending a resume. Any good third party can help ensure that your letter and resume are directed at the right branches of the decision tree.

Using third parties to make your calls or to forward letters is a special technique, one to be used only in situations where you are unable to get through on your own or where the job target is in a new field and you need extra help.

Conveying Benefits by Phone

Your presentation of yourself and of the qualities and skills you embody could take a little practice. Write a short personal bio in relation to the kinds of work you are interested in, and then memorize it. Speak *from* it not *about* it. Make a list of powerful questions you can ask. Ask questions that show you have been thinking. Ask for permission: "Hello, my name is Tom Jackson; may I have five minutes of your time to ask a professional question?"

Note: Be sure to make the distinction between calls to get leads and referrals and those to get an interview. Separate employers from whom you want information from those you want to meet. Call honestly and address the listener's interests as much as your own. Listen to what is said and take notes.

The phone presentation must be concise. Don't try to explain a complicated mechanical process in a phone call. You can do that in the interview. To get an interview talk about the payoff you offer.

□ Your lead-in statement should be strong and short.
□ The payoff should be within reason. Don't promise to double profits in thirty days . . . even if you can!
□ The payoff should be measurable rather than a self-evaulation. Don't say "I'm very good at . . ."; instead, say "On my most recent assignment, sales went up for three quarters in a row," "There are three patents pending . . . ," "I'll bring in some sample designs . . . ," or "Our client list grew by 20 percent."

Try to learn at least the basic jargon of your job target. If you've been in the field you'll know these terms automatically. If you're changing fields and have done your research in depth, you'll have picked up the lingo from magazines, journals, and talking to people. Listen, and take notes.

Put yourself in place of an employer listening to the following telephone lead-in statements. Do they work from the standpoint of possible benefits to the listener?

Hi. This is Roger Wey. I'm a graduate of Penn State and have a master's degree in finance, and would like to have an interview. Can you see me?

Hello. This is Sally Holly calling. I wonder if I could stop by to discuss a possible position with your company?

Hello. I'm sorry to bother you but I'm looking for a job in packaging design and thought you might have something. Do you?

They don't work at all. Nothing Roger, Sally, or Nameless said conveyed a real benefit to the potential employer. All seemed slightly grasping. They also left it to the potential employer to try to figure out what use, if any, they might possibly be to the firm, even if there were an opening.

Compare those statements with these:

Hi, Mr. Borden. This is Roger Wey. I understand that you have recently expanded your cost control section and I'd like to talk with you about some research I did for my master's degree in finance. I think it might be quite relevant to what you are doing. I wonder if I could stop by for a few minutes to meet you.

Hello. This is Sally Holly calling, is this Miss Kavaliascus? Good. I wanted to talk with you about some work I've been doing in pattern design that I think would fit in well with your new look in coats. Could I stop by next Monday morning and show you the samples?

Hello. Mr. Wade? This is Pat Turner. Ted Casey suggested that I call you about a series of new package designs I've put together. I think they could be adaptable to the new nutritional milkshake product you're planning to market.

Positive Attitude

You must believe an employer will hire you *anytime, anyplace,* regardless of the unemployment rate, if you can show him that you have a positive value to offer—a benefit which is related to the company's needs and which will bring in a high yield on the investment of hiring you.

PRACTICE EXERCISE

Prepare a three-minute statement that will be so persuasive that the person at the other end of the line will invite you in for a meeting.

PRE-CALLING CHECKLIST

Pick a prospective employer target and describe the firm's biggest needs related to what you can contribute.

Employer Name_____

Needs_____

_____

_____

_____

Describe the job target for which you're calling to get an interview.

_____

_____

_____

_____

Conveying Benefits by Mail

An effective employment inquiry or resume needs an attention-getting lead or cover letter. This requires one or two short paragraphs that compellingly state the benefits you offer (see chapter 15, step 9).

Here are a few benefit-oriented paragraphs:

After three years of concentrated effort on my part we had 150 new maintenance accounts. This was twice what Central Services had. It is possible I could do the same for your group and would like to meet with you if you are interested.

My design decreased fuel costs by 15 percent and helped turn the industry upside down. I have some comparable ideas that might fit your situation.

The bank had never been on local television before. It was the best thing that could have happened to them.

I helped build what was a three-person department—including myself—to one that now is staffed by thirty-five people doing research and responsible for the company's major marketing decisions.

Now it's your turn. Write the opening paragraph for a cover letter you might send with your resume to an employer target.

_____

_____

_____

_____

_____

Closing the Call

There are some people who can make great presentations but cannot close a deal. They don't know how to wrap it up—whether the deal is a legal contract, a real estate sale, or an interview. Many an applicant has done a superb self-selling job only to finish with an inane remark, such as "Anyway, if you ever happen to have the time sometime, maybe we could get together again." Always make it a point to have a closing request ready: "When can we talk again?" or "Would it be possible for us to meet?"

MEETING OBJECTIONS

Throughout your career voyage you'll meet people who aren't quite as eager to meet you as you are to meet them. You'll come face-to-face with the reasons why they can't do what you want. These reasons are *objections*.

Listen to these objections, and then, instead of just turning away, see if you can counter the objection—not with an argument but with a logical reason that the employer should consider what you want anyway. Look at the following examples:

> PROSPECTIVE
> EMPLOYER: Well that sounds great. Why don't you send over a resume?
>
> YOU: I could drop off a copy myself.
>
> P.E.: We're supposed to go through personnel.
>
> YOU: Oh, I understand. Why don't I see you first, and then drop off another copy with them.
>
> P.E.: I'm jammed up with meetings.
>
> YOU: I could come by at five. Maybe we could have a quick coffee?
>
> P.E.: You know we're not hiring right now. In fact, we're cutting back.
>
> YOU: That's why I called. I've some sound ideas on how to accomplish with ten people what you've been doing with twenty, and maintain the volume.

How might you overcome the following objections:

P.E.: Send us a resume.

YOU_____

_____

_____

_____

P.E.: I'll be out of town for about three weeks.

YOU_____

_____

_____

_____

P.E.: The department budget for new employees has been cut. There's really not much point.

YOU_____

_____

_____

P.E.: We won't be hiring until next spring—why not contact me then?
You_____

_____

_____

_____

P.E.: OK, you win. Come in for an interview.
You_____

_____

_____

_____

SPECIAL STRATEGIES FOR GETTING INSIDE

□

Over the years we've encountered many unique and creative ideas that job-seekers have employed to get themselves inside ahead of the crowd. Some were so outlandish that they backfired. Others were not only creative, but got the job-seeker his or her job target. Here are two inventive techniques that worked.

The Come-on Ad

John X pretended to be an employer. He inserted a blind box-number ad in his local newspaper, describing the position he would have liked to find for himself. The responses he got provided him with much useful information.

It identified people who had left or were planning to leave their jobs. Properly interpreted, this information revealed a list of job openings.

It also gave him an overview of salary levels and responsibilities that related to his own campaign.

It identified a variety of employers that applicants had worked for before their present jobs which were also potential targets for him.

It even identified a company in which he had been particularly interested. He had no idea that there might be an opening there but the response to the ad indirectly informed him that a key employee was planning to leave.

Breaking the Box-Number Code

The difficulty in responding to box-number advertisements is that you don't know who the organization is, unless (and until) they are interested in you. This makes it almost impossible to do the kind of research essential to an aggressive approach.

Henrietta Y used the following rather simple approach to these ads: Using her brother-in-law's name, she wrote a fictitious letter-style resume, exactly in line with the advertised requirements for the position. Her brother-in-law got an immediate response on company letterhead and gave it to Henrietta. She then approached the company directly, never indicating that she knew there was an opening, and sold herself into a successful interview.

14

□

THE POWER RESUME

An Advertisement for Yourself

Over the years we've talked to hundreds of employers, managers, supervisors, job counselors, placement agents, and personnel people. Here are some of the critiques we've heard about resumes:

If a resume is too long and wordy, I don't read it. I simply don't have the time to try to figure out what they're *trying* to tell me.

I make a real effort to read every resume I receive. But my eyes blur at some of the involved sentences, circuitous reasoning, and lack of any evidence of coherent thinking I often see on resumes. How can I hire somebody to write reports when she can't even explain to me clearly who she is and what she can do?

I dislike wordy, flowery, life history resumes. I also have a pet peeve about bad spelling and typing and about colored paper. When a person is looking for a $30,000-or-more-a-year job, the resume should look like the applicant is worth the money.

A good cover letter is very important in persuading me to read the resume. When I see a printed cover letter that says "I am sincerely interested in working for your company," I think, What kind of a fool does this person think I am? How many other companies did he send this valentine to?

A good way to practice resume writing is to practice ad writing. Here's an exercise to give you the feel of the technique without much effort. Pretend to be an employer, and write an employment ad for your selected job-target position. Write fifty words or fewer (remember, words cost money). Assume the ad will run in the classified section of your Sunday paper. Try to make clear every point that you think would be important in describing the position.

Now look at what you wrote. Are there words you could eliminate? Facts that could be stated more clearly? Edit. Clean up. Cut it down. Remember, it's always harder to be concise. And your audience doesn't have much time to figure out what you want to say.

Resume writing is an art. It is probably the most important and neglected of all the arts of business communication. Top mail-order writers who can sell anything from real estate to rock candy suddenly develop writer's cramp when they have to sell themselves in a resume. In the job market, where a good resume can be the most vital of all instruments for making prime contact, people continue to approach resume writing incorrectly, halfheartedly, and often with resentment.

What is a resume? It's not an autobiography. Nor is it your memoir. A resume is an advertisement for yourself. It is an ad selling *you*. The purpose of this ad is to get you an interview. No more, no less. It's the interview that can get you the job. All the resume can do is get you invited in. During the interview you can fill in any details you think are appropriate to the particular position.

Usually, a resume is aimed at a general job area, rather than at a specific employer. In some cases a resume may be written specifically for a particular company and even a particular position within that company. This is an excellent self-selling approach and an extremely effective one. However, it is not practical in all cases, because of the obvious time and effort involved in personalizing as many as one hundred resumes. This is where the cover letter is put to use.

TEN STEPS TO AN INTERVIEW-GETTING RESUME

□

On the following pages we will take you through an organized, proven procedure for preparing a compelling resume that will get you in for interviews. This is a step-by-step approach that has been distilled from hundreds of hours of work with individuals and their resumes. Please follow each step carefully and participate to the best of your ability.

Step 1. Take the Employer's Point of View

Review your job target again, this time from the point of view of your future employer. Say to yourself, I am Mr. or Ms. B. and I would like to hire someone to:

_____

(Write in your job target.)

Now, complete the statements below from the employer's point of view. Once you get the feel of your potential employer's needs, you have a far better chance of communicating with her successfully.

1. I want a person who knows how to perform the following specific tasks:

    _____
    _____
    _____
    _____

2. I want a person who has had some of the following experience:

    _____
    _____
    _____
    _____

3. If he or she didn't have the specific experience, I believe I would hire a person who could convince me that he or she had the following equivalent abilities:

    _____
    _____
    _____
    _____

4. I want a person with the following personal qualities:

    _____
    _____
    _____
    _____

5. I must have a person who can solve the following kinds of problems for me:

_____

_____

_____

_____

How did you like being the employer? Were you able to complete each statement easily and precisely? If you were, you should be able to write a forceful resume. But if you were like most employers, filling in the responses wasn't that easy. Were you a bit unsure? Most employers are. Employers often have as much difficulty in deciding exactly what they are looking for as you have in describing exactly who you are and what you can do.

Nevertheless, no matter how murky and obscure an employer may be about the specific abilities, experience, or personality traits that she might like to find in a new employee, *she almost always knows exactly what problems she wants her employee to solve.* That's what work is all about—solving problems. This is a vitally important point to always keep in mind.

And that's why statements 1 and 5 are the most crucial ones on the above list. Reread them. If you've responded only partially or not at all, think about it. Try very hard now to answer fully and completely. What are the tasks and problems that an employer in your job-target area would want performed and solved?

Your value as a potential employee depends on how well you can convince an employer that you have the ability to solve the problems she needs to have solved. The guiding principle in preparing your resume should be defining and enhancing those problem-solving skills that relate to your job target in a way that conveys a benefit to a potential employer.

This principle holds true in good times and bad, boom or recession. If your resume can convince an employer that hiring you is an asset, you will get an interview. The next step could be the job you want.

Step 2. Taking a Personal Inventory

In our experience, one of the most common mistakes resume writers make is to start right out in the upper left-hand corner of a blank sheet of paper and keep writing until the final period in the lower right-hand corner.

As an aid, fill out the Resume Preplanning Form below. This will provide an inventory of your skills, accomplishments, education, work history, and other facts about yourself. This form will help you recall important information that you can use when the time comes to write the actual resume. Filling it out takes extra time, but it pays extra dividends.

RESUME PREPLANNING FORM

□

Education

HIGH SCHOOL

Year graduated _____
Specialization _____
Favorite subjects_____
_____

Best general areas (writing, speaking, acting, sports, politics, etc.)
_____
_____

Hobbies from high school that continued to develop later
_____
_____

Proudest accomplishments

□ _____
□ _____
□ _____

Work experience
_____
_____
_____

COLLEGE

Years attended _____ Degrees_____
Grade point average_____
Honors (if any)_____
Major field _____
Favorite subjects_____
_____
Why?_____
_____
Your most significant academic achievements_____
_____
_____
Your three most significant nonacademic achievements while in college
1. _____
2. _____
3. _____
Work experience while in college
_____
_____
_____
Extracurricular activities while at college
_____
_____
_____
Elected offices at college (if any)
_____
_____
Athletic achievements at college (if any)
_____
_____
Other significant accomplishments in college
_____
_____
_____
Other education or training (include vocational, military, corporate, schools, correspondence courses, etc.)

Course	School	Skills

Hobbies and Interests

List your hobbies or interests and indicate degree of proficiency.

	Proficiency	
	Excellent	Good

Do you see any work application of your hobbies and interests with or without further training? _____ Yes _____ No
If yes, explain _____
_____
_____
_____

Military Service (if applicable)

Branch of service_____

Rank (highest attained)_____

Total years_____

List any special schools attended _____

_____

_____

What were your major military functions?_____

_____

_____

_____

Describe any skills you acquired in the military that might have some commercial application._____

_____

_____

_____

_____

Special Skills

These are skills you've developed over your life from any and all sources. Indicate your degree of proficiency in each area. List additional skills as applicable.

COMMUNICATION SKILLS

Proficiency

Skill	Excellent	Good	Application to Work
Writing			
Talking			
Selling			
Teaching			
Organizing			
Supervising			
Motivating			
Analysis			

Languages: Rate your proficiency in any foreign languages by a 1, 2, or 3—1 being the highest level.

Language	Speak	Read	Write

CREATIVE SKILLS

Proficiency

Skill	Excellent	Good	Application to Work
Painting			
Composing			
Writing			
Designing			
Acting			
Innovating			
Programming			
Other crafts			

INTELLECTUAL SKILLS

Proficiency

Skill	Excellent	Good	Application to Work
Studying			
Researching			
Analyzing			
Organizing			
Problem solving			
Decision making			
Planning			

Job-Related Accomplishments

The purpose of this section of the Resume Preplanning Form is to make an inventory of your *work* successes, your best job accomplishments. This need not be done in chronological order.

Describe a number of work/job accomplishments, if possible equal to the number of years of your working experience (describe five if you've worked five years, fifteen if you've worked fifteen years, etc.). Each accomplishment need not be in a separate year. State position, employer, and year of each accomplishment. Accomplishments should relate to areas like profits or sales, increased efficiency, improved human relations, better designs, finer acoustics, or whatever it was in your job area that generally promoted and enriched your work product and/or contributed directly to the well-being of the company or individual client.

Year	Employer & Position	Accomplishment

Have you ever had supervisory responsibilities? _____ Yes _____ No

If yes, describe scope, number of people supervised, their levels, and type of operation for each recent instance of supervision.

1. _____
_____
_____

2. _____
_____

3. _____
_____

Non-Work-Related Skills

Include only problem-solving skills that are generally *outside* of previous or present jobs.

1. _____
2. _____
3. _____
4. _____
5. _____
6. _____
7. _____
8. _____
9. _____
10. _____

SUMMARY

Now that you have listed skills and accomplishments from the past, the more recent past, and the present, look back over the Resume Preplanning Form and the earlier list from the Skill/Interest Cross Index on page 53. In each space below write a short paragraph summarizing those skills and accomplishments you think would be most applicable to your current job target.

Skills

_____
_____
_____

_____
_____

Accomplishments
_____
_____
_____
_____

Step 3. Find the Right Words—Convey Benefits

A resume is a presentation in words. Your aim in writing a resume is to convey immediate meaning and to suggest a benefit to your potential employer. Therefore, you must use words with strong impact. Avoid such phrases as: "I was responsible for . . . ," "My duties involved . . . ," "Project manager," "Assistant manager," "Staff coordinator," etc. Instead, use *action words*. Action words convey a sense of participation, involvement, and accomplishment. Here's a sample list of some action words:

designed	researched	trained
supervised	directed	reduced
implemented	analyzed	invented
developed	planned	managed
created	organized	negotiated
conducted	sold	wrote
expanded	increased	presented

ACCOMPLISHMENT VERSUS INFORMATION

An accomplishment is an action that produced a final beneficial result. Information is simply a statement of fact, such as a description of duties, job title, etc.; it does not transmit the feeling of something achieved. Both sets of data are highly valid in a resume; however, real accomplishment statements are far better for selling you. Look at these examples:

INFORMATION ORIENTED
I was responsible for the organization and management of the entire Art Department. Hired and supervised designers, commercial artists, and print specialists.

ACCOMPLISHMENT ORIENTED

Directed eight persons in Art Department. Designed 22 product brochures, which contributed to increasing sales by 50 percent in major market areas. Cut print production costs by 25 percent.

INFORMATION ORIENTED

I was the Assistant to the Curator at the museum. My duties involved coordinating membership drives, meeting visiting dignitaries, planning and organizing events and schedules, assembling reports, and some secretarial duties.

ACCOMPLISHMENT ORIENTED

As Assistant Curator, handled an average of 14 special museum functions each month. Coordinated four major membership drives which each added more than 500 new members. Originated and laid out two outdoor projects which received national acclaim.

We repeat: A resume is an advertisement for yourself. Follow these rules in preparing this important ad:

- ☐ Use the minimum number of words necessary to convey your meaning.
- ☐ Avoid "wind up" words and phrases such as "My duties included . . ." or "I was in charge of the section that . . ." Start right out with precise action words and benefits.
- ☐ Use short sentences. Don't try to convey too many ideas at once.
- ☐ Be sure your punctuation and spelling are correct.
- ☐ Don't be overtechnical. Most resumes go through personnel first.
- ☐ Leave out data that are not relevant to getting you an interview.

READ BEFORE YOU WRITE

Before you start writing your resume, it is a good idea to familiarize yourself with a number of job advertisements in your field of interest. The words and phrases used by prospective employers in these ads may give you a clearer idea of what they are looking for. If few ads relating to your job target are readily at hand, look at back issues of trade publications in your field.

Step 4. Select the Best Format

You are now ready to start organizing your resume. More accurately, you will organize the information in a way that will help ensure that it is read.

There are three generally recognized formats or organizational styles for resumes, each with its own advantages and disadvantages: chronological, functional, and combination. A fourth format we have devised is the targeted resume.

CHRONOLOGICAL RESUME

This is the most widely used resume format, and the one with which employers are more familiar. It is also the easiest to write. Jobs are listed chronologically, starting with the most recent. The most recent employment usually occupies the most space—although this is not necessary, particularly where this experience is not related to your current job target or the job has been of short duration.

Dates of employment are given first, followed by name of employer and your job title. For each position you held, start a new paragraph describing accomplishments on that job. You usually are expected to give both month and year of employment, but if you had a period of unemployment that you want to bury, you can normally get by with including just the years. In that case, however, you should be prepared to talk about these gaps at the interview.

Some advantages of the chronological resume are:

□ Professional interviewers are most familiar with it.
□ It is the easiest to prepare because its content is structured by familiar dates, companies, and titles.
□ It can emphasize a steady employment record (when there has been little job hopping).

Some disadvantages of the chronological resume are:

□ It starkly reveals serious employment gaps.
□ It can put undesired emphasis on job areas that you might prefer to ignore.
□ It makes it difficult to spotlight particular areas of skills and accomplishment unless they are in most recent jobs.

FUNCTIONAL RESUME

The functional resume categorizes your work into specific categories of experience or skill that you wish to highlight for a specific job target. It gives little or no regard to when and where experience was attained.

Some advantages of the functional resume:

- It stresses selected areas of accomplishment and experience that might be most marketable in your job target.
- It helps camouflage a spotty employment record or one with little actual experience in the job-target area.
- It allows you to show real professional growth in desired areas.
- It is a useful way to play down work areas that you wish to deemphasize.

Some disadvantages of the functional resume are:

- Some employers are slightly suspicious of it and will want to see more specific work history information.
- It is difficult to stress corporate or organization affiliations.
- It is harder for an interviewer to follow.

COMBINATION RESUME

This combination resume resembles a basic functional resume, but with the addition of a list of company names and dates.

The combination format allows you the best of both worlds. You can stress the skill areas that are most relevant to you while satisfying the employer's need to know names and dates. Titles should be included with the company listings; however, if they are not in keeping with the job target, they can be left off without much negative effect.

Some advantages of the combination format are:

- It gives you the opportunity to emphasize valued skills and abilities.
- It helps cushion the impact of gaps in employment.
- It can be varied by increasing the chronology portion and decreasing the functional portion, or vice versa.

Some disadvantages of the combination format are:

- It tends to run longer than the other two forms.
- Since it takes longer to read, the employer can lose interest.

TARGETED RESUME

This format has gained popularity since it was introduced by this author in 1981 in *The Perfect Resume*. To use a targeted resume you should have a well-focused, fully researched job target. Unlike the other resume formats, which feature an affirmative picture of past history, the targeted resume features a series of statements concerning what *you can do* (your capabilities), whether or not you actually have had direct, relevant experience.

The design is extremely easy to follow. You name your specific job target at the top of the page. The next major block of space (about 30 percent) is a list of capabilities, or specifics on what you can do in that target area. The next block is a list of accomplishments, proven facts from your past work or life history that support your ability to execute the demands of that job target. The last section is a chronological work history—dates, companies, and titles. Education is listed at the bottom.

Some advantages of the targeted resume are:

□   You can fully exploit and demonstrate your knowledge and potential of a specific job target.
□   You can custom design the resume to several different targets.
□   You can emphasize capabilities you possess for which you may not yet have been paid.

Some disadvantages of the targeted resume are:

□   You still leave questions regarding a complete detail of your past work history.
□   You generally can't do even a small mailing, since your resume's focus is narrow.
□   You must have real experience of some kind to back up the capabilities statements (otherwise, the resume is hollow and based only on potential).

WHICH RESUME SHOULD YOU USE?

Consider your own employment history. How many jobs have you had? What do you wish to emphasize? Are there any gaps you want to soften? Are you changing fields?

Study the examples we have provided. If you have difficulty in deciding which format to use, you might want to draft a resume in each format and then decide. Once you've selected a format, it's time to move on to drafting the resume.

CHRONOLOGICAL RESUME

□

This is a typical chronological resume. Shows major responsibilities and diversity of experience. No gaps.

Diane Tims

800 Main Street
Portland, Oregon 97208
503-555-5523

ADMINISTRATIVE ASSISTANT

Work Experience:
1991 - 1993

Administrative Assistant to Chairman –
University of Oregon, Department of Psychology

- Ran day-to-day operations of 15-person department.
- Created liaison corps with central university administration offices.
- Organized university and government surveys and reports.
- Increased efficiency by 30% in two years.
- Set up agenda and recorded faculty meeting minutes.
- Prepared authorizations of expenditures of $675,000 budget.
- Prepared quantity audits, projections, and financial statements.
- Interpreted and applied university and government policies.

1989 - 1991

Secretary to Chairman of Physics Department –
Portland State University

- Carried out administrative policies of section – processing payroll, coordinating work schedules, ordering supplies and equipment.
- Scheduled meetings and appointments.

1978 - 1989

Assistant to Editor, *Journal of Applied Physics*

- Responsible for day-to-day journal operation, handling all general queries regarding journal, communication with authors, referees, and publisher, preparation of statistics, agenda, and minutes of editors' meetings.

Education:

B.A. Portland State University, 1978
Humanities major. Honor student.

FUNCTIONAL RESUME

□

Mr. Moran does not show names and dates of employers. His work record is somewhat spotty (four jobs in six years), so it is advantageous to present his background in a functional format.

James Moran
3 Hemlock Drive
Silver Spring, Md. 20904
301-555-5944

DESIGN & DEVELOPMENT

Designed and developed four large-scale communications systems. Performed studies for application of digital techniques to telephone networks. Analyzed digital multiple-access discrete-address system for use in satellite communications.

Analyzed the effectiveness of modulation and error-encoding techniques against atmospheric-type noise. Cited by Engineering Society for Inventive Creations, 1988. Other contributions were in the design of digital communications systems using different types of modulation techniques.

COMPUTER SYSTEMS ANALYSIS

Analyzed data from various test systems on secret military equipment and wrote programs for computerization. Planned and designed diagnostic systems for on-line real-time computer.

DATA ANALYSIS

Analyzed data from planned tests to see if systems performed according to theoretical determinations. Analyzed data from six different test systems and prepared reports. Responsible for integration and reduction of special trajectory analysis data.

EDUCATION

MSEE -- George Washington University, 1989
BSEE -- Columbia University, 1984, Information Theory & Coding
BS -- University of Maryland, 1980

COMBINATION RESUME

Because his experience is chiefly with one firm, it is best for this applicant to use a combined chronological-functional resume. It highlights his experience with Acton and only touches on the earlier experience (which at this time in his career is not significant).

Jack E. Nelson
1000 21 Street, N.W.
Ft. Lauderdale, Fla. 33308
303-555-8193

SALES MANAGEMENT: Responsible for planning and directing sales program for several companies. Made major policy decisions as to all phases of sales activities. Successfully built sales 85 percent above preceding year's business.

MARKETING PLANNING: Investigated the market for new products and new markets for established product lines. Introduced new chewing gum package to supermarkets after market study indicating need.

MERCHANDISING: Developed point-of-purchase displays that gave added shelf space to company products and increased sales. Coordinated merchandising and advertising programs with stores. Developed new packaging concepts that made company products outstanding seller in frozen food cabinets.

SALES TRAINING: Hired and trained large crew of merchandisers and salespeople. Set up formal program to train them in company product and sales techniques. Wrote sales-training manuals.

SALES: Maintained close personal contact with buyers in major supermarket outlets. Personally sold products to chains all over the U.S.

ACTON CHEWING GUM COMPANY
Sales Manager – 1979 – 1991
Started as a salesman and worked through sales ranks to current position in 1988.

BEST'S CANDY COMPANY
Salesman – 1970 – 1979
Sold candy to supermarkets, drug variety chains, and vending machine companies.

EDUCATION: B.A., Florida State College, 1970.

TARGETED RESUME
□

DAVID C. HALPERN
6200 Pershing Road
Chicago, IL 60609
312-555-0917

JOB TARGET: INTERNATIONAL SALES OR MARKETING MANAGER

CAPABILITIES:

- Market and sell industrial and agricultural chemicals.
- Direct and coordinate activities concerned with research and development of new concepts and basic data on an organization's products, services, or ideologies.
- Plan and formulate all aspects of projects, applications to be utilized from findings, and costs – including equipment and manpower requirements.
- Approve and submit proposals considered feasible to management for consideration and allocation of funds.
- Develop and implement monitoring methods and procedures such as project reports and staff conferences.
- Negotiate contracts with consulting firms to perform studies.
- Achieve competitive edge through effective use of know-how in product coordination, ship chartering, insurance, and letters of credit.

ACHIEVEMENTS:

- Managed cost analyses pertinent to specific products and countries in relation to total consumption, pricing, competitors, market share, local production facilities, freighting, and credit.
- Successfully gained market information through agents, distributors, and international government agencies.
- Arranged sensitive offshore deals and "swap-out material" with competitors in Europe, the Far East and Latin America.
- Sold industrial packaging materials to numerous Fortune 500 corporations.
- Increased market share of an industrial paper product from 27% to 31% in six-month period.

WORK HISTORY:

1984-Present	INTERNATIONAL CHEMICALS COMPANY – Chicago, IL.
	Trader, Trading Division
	Product Manager, Chemical Group
1981-1984	CROWN ZELLERBACH CORPORATION – San Francisco, CA.
	Sales Representative, Industrial Packaging
1975-1981	AMERICAN EXPORT SHIPPING – San Francisco, CA
	Vessel Navigator

EDUCATION: STANFORD UNIVERSITY – M.B.A. International Business, 1984

Step 5. Prepare a First Draft

We're ready to write . . . but only a first draft. Don't even attempt to make your resume look good on the first try—it won't work.

Begin with the idea that you are going to make at least two or three constantly improved drafts before you have a resume that is easy to read, has an attractive layout, conveys distinct benefits, and makes the person it goes to want to interview you.

HOW TO PREPARE THE FIRST DRAFT OF YOUR RESUME

NOTE: If possible, get access to a word processor or a computer with some resume software. Make full use of the best technology you can find to write your resume. Make a specific version for each employer; save each version on disk.

1. Get several sheets of blank paper or prepare different working documents on the computer or word processor. Each page or document should contain one position you have had, or one skill or work function you wish to emphasize. Education and any other information you want to include should also be drafted on separate pieces of paper or documents.

2. Reread the Resume Preplanning Form and extract from it the dates, names, positions, accomplishments, and problem-solving capabilities you wish to emphasize. Write this information down on the appropriate sheets (or enter in the appropriate document). Then add to this information any facts or accomplishments that can further improve your image. Remember to list facts in accomplishment terms and to use action words that convey information as concisely as possible.

3. Look at the phrases and comments you have written, and organize each into concise paragraphs. Concentrate on each area separately, paragraph by paragraph, rewriting and editing as often as necessary until the ideas are conveyed in the cleanest, briefest, and most forceful form.

4. Now combine the paragraphs into a full chronological, functional, or combination resume. Type or print this out, single spaced, on one or two sheets of paper. If too long, edit it again. Make sure that the information is well written and concise, and that it communicates valid benefits to the potential employer. Check spelling and punctuation carefully. For

the targeted resume, you should write down twenty to thirty capabilities statements—things you can do in that targeted field. Then eliminate the least important statements. Boil it down to the top six or seven statements and rewrite them to your highest standards.

Step 6. Edit and Critique

A good resume is virtually guaranteed by a thorough critical appraisal and careful editing and rewriting. This rewriting is aimed at reorganizing your resume in such a way that it will come alive for your prospective reader. You have three objectives relating to form and content:

1. *The elimination of extraneous information.* The longer the resume, the less chance that all the information will be absorbed by the reader. This fact should be kept constantly in mind as you edit your second draft and plan the third rewrite. Most experts suggest you aim for a one-page presentation. Here are some items that generally do not belong in a resume, and simply take up space:

    □ Number of children
    □ Marital status
    □ Religion
    □ Sex
    □ Age
    □ Race
    □ Health
    □ Maiden name
    □ Spouse's occupation
    □ Social clubs
    □ College fraternities
    □ Hobbies (unless relevant to the job you want)
    □ Courses studied for which no credit was given (unless relevant)
    □ Languages (unless relevant to the job)
    □ References

2. *An attractive layout.* You will want to be certain that the layout—margins, spacing, use of underlining, headings, and white space—results in a clear presentation, one that is both forceful and inviting (more about layout in step 7).

3.   *A strong writing style.* You want to be confident that the writing style is direct, interesting, and accomplishment-oriented.

THE PROCESS OF CRITIQUING

Once you have completed your second draft—in the format and approximate layout you've picked—it's time to look for more objective views. The outside critique of family, friends, trusted colleagues, or a placement counselor is imperative. Often this essential step is ignored because you feel you have done a good enough job. Or because you don't want to bother anyone. Or you have reservations about involving others in a private matter such as a resume.

While we sympathize with these feelings, intelligent feedback from reliable people is the best way to ensure that your resume does the job it is supposed to do—that it conveys an attractive, convincing picture of your capabilities.

There is an art to obtaining a good critique. You don't simply turn the resume over to a friend and say "Hey, take a look at this. Do you think it's any good?" Most people don't like to criticize others, especially friends, and will probably reply with something like "It looks good to me." Therefore, your request for criticism must be made in a way that elicits valuable feedback.

Have the individual read the resume once or twice and then ask her to put it down and describe what she learned about you. The response will be the overall impression gained through the resume. This procedure is more valid when carried out with someone who doesn't know you too well.

Ask for criticism in terms of *improvement*—"Would you mind giving me some ideas about how I can make this resume more effective?" Review your critic's general observations, and then focus on specific questions such as: "Do you think the resume could be shortened?" "How would you improve the layout?" "Is the format clear?" "Do I give enough information about my abilities?"

Step 7. Design an Attractive Layout

Remember our analogy of the resume as an advertisement. One of the first criteria for a good advertisement is an attractive layout. A presentation that looks good—with the right amount of type for the space and with proper margins—will immediately draw the eye to the important points.

Your potential interviewer is inundated with paperwork. He or she must absorb and digest hundreds of pages of printed information each week—not only resumes, but reports, memoranda, technical papers, etc. What happens to your resume when it lands on top of this pile of paper?

Obviously, it could be ignored. When you lay out your resume, visualize it in the middle of a fairly high stack of other resumes and papers. It's around 4:00 P.M., your reader is tired—his eyes hurt, his blood sugar is a bit low, he needs a vacation—and he's read thirty-four resumes that day and only four or five of passing interest. Do you wish you could retrieve your resume? Get it back and have it retyped on a high quality word processor (laser printed), allow for wider margins, capitalize some key words, eliminate extraneous words, take out two whole paragraphs. In short, make it easier to read.

After you've boiled your resume down to the most concise forceful expression of your skills and experience, emphasize the information you want to convey by creative *but very conservative* use of capital letters, underlining, and spacing.

Keep in mind the final look of your resume. Pay attention to paragraph length and spacing. A top-heavy first paragraph is unattractive. No paragraphs should be bulky. It's better to have two short paragraphs than one heavy one.

Give less space to job experience that does not fit your current job target.

If a second page must be used, make sure the key information is on the first page.

Step 8. Typing and Printing

Use a top quality word processor and laser printer with a clean, clear typeface.* If you don't type, pay someone to prepare the final proof. Have someone else proofread for spelling and grammar errors. Then, take this final version to a good local printer (check the yellow pages) and order one hundred copies on a good but not extravagant grade of paper. The cost will be nominal compared to the benefits you will get from a well-prepared resume. Use off-white or buff stock. Keep the original clean and flat, in case

---

* Many of the software kits on the market for the preparation of resumes will do an excellent job. We recommend *The Perfect Resume Computer Kit* by this author and Bill Buckingham. Information can be obtained from Permax Systems, Inc., Box 6455, Madison, WI 53716; telephone 800-233-6460.

you need to reprint. If you are using a computer and laser printer, you can customize each resume. Avoid photocopiers unless they are of the highest quality and the machine can print on good quality stock.

If you use a commercial resume service, make sure that they follow your layout, or that you specifically agree to any changes which they suggest.

Step 9. The Cover Letter

A cover letter accompanying a resume is your personal introduction to a potential employer. It encourages the employer to read your resume. As good as it is, the resume is a printed form that focuses on your skills and experience in a given area. It is meant to be read by many potential employers. The cover letter relates the information in your resume to the *specific* needs of the employer. It is meant to be read by one potential employer. If you are sending a resume to fifteen different potential employers, you will write fifteen different cover letters. Each letter will have a somewhat different slant on how your skills relate to that employer's needs.

Therefore, each cover letter must be custom-made; it should be the result of some investigation into the specific problems that a specific employer needs solved. You can sometimes deduce these problems from an article in a trade journal, from general information, or through gossip about the company or the person. Or you can take an educated guess, and mix it with common sense. But whatever you do, the cover letter should be sufficiently personalized to compel the reader to look at your resume.

Three elements are involved in writing good cover letters:

First, address the letter, using name and title (double check spelling), to the particular person with whom you wish to have an interview.

Second, refer to a problem-solving skill that will be further expanded in your resume, one that can provide a direct benefit to this employer.

Third, the closing is as important as the opening. Try to suggest an interview time. Here are some examples of how to close a letter:

I would like to meet with you briefly on August 15, and will contact your secretary to see if this date is open or what an alternative date might be.

Because of travel plans, I will be available for interview only during the next two weeks. I hope we can meet. I'll give you a call.

I would like to stop by some day next week to show you an actual model of the new program.

In addition, the cover letter should be nor more than three paragraphs long (half a page, centered). Use personal letterhead (if you don't have any, get some printed at the same place that printed your resume). Type your cover letter or use a word processor. If you are responding to an advertisement, try to use some of the words from the ad in your letter.

SAMPLE COVER LETTER
□

June 18, 1992

Dr. Robert Sayers
President
Seattle Community College
12 Rocky Mt. Road
Seattle, Washington 98101

Dear Dr. Sayers:

My firsthand experience in the administrative staffs of two colleges should be of interest to you in your new drive to centralize administrative functions of SCC.

The enclosed resume will give you the highlights of my experience in handling the specific administrative problems of college departments. Of special interest is turning over forty years of filing to an easy-access data base in a record-breaking six months (including a complete staff training).

We are moving to Seattle at the end of this school year. I will be in your city from April 10 to 24. If possible, I would like to arrange an appointment during that period to discuss your new organization, and explain how my experience might be beneficial. I will call you to clear this.

Yours very truly,

Diane Tims

Enc: resume

SAMPLE COVER LETTER

□

James Moran
3 Hemlock Drive
Silver Spring, Md. 20904
301-555-5944

March 6, 1992

Mr. Wayne J. Anthony
Director of Engineering
Aztec Electronics Co.
70 Circle Drive
Rockville, Md. 20850

Dear Mr. Anthony:

I read in yesterday's "Electronics" about your new contract for manufacturing parallel access discrete communications systems.

I have worked on the development of similar systems for the Computronics Corporation and feel that this experience could make a direct and immediate contribution. Details are in the enclosed resume.

I would like the opportunity to discuss this with you sometime next week if possible. I'll contact you shortly to explore a possible meeting time.

Sincerely,

James Moran

Enc: resume

COVER LETTER TO
EXECUTIVE RECRUITING FIRM

□

May 2, 1992

Mr. Maxwell Harper
President
Harper Associates, Inc.
22 W. 48th Street
New York, New York 10036

Dear Mr. Harper:

You were recommended to me by Alan Botson at CBS.

Perhaps one of your clients can use a successful sales manager with a strong, proven track record and with heavy background in consumer packaged goods.

I know and am known by purchasing and merchandising executives in the major food, drug, and variety chains throughout the East. They can attest to my accomplishments.

Since Acton, my present employer, is to be acquired by Rogers and Barley, Ltd., I feel this is a good time to make a move. My current salary is in the low 70s, plus a bonus and car.

My resume is enclosed. Please keep me in mind for positions anywhere in the country where my experience will be of value. I will contact you shortly to get acquainted.

Sincerely,

Jack E. Nelson

COVER LETTER
FOR TARGETED RESUME

February 27, 1993

Mr. A. Bramford West
Senior Vice President, Marketing
Blackmun-Hargood Manufacturing
11587 Southfield Avenue
Parsippany, NJ 07054

Dear Mr. West:

I've carefully studied the recent *Wall Street Journal* and *Business Week* analyses of your fiber optics expansion, and feel certain my specific skills and talents would be a big plus to your newly organized team.

As my resume indicates, I've had extensive marketing experience worldwide, including seven years arranging deals with Japanese investors and manufacturers. In addition, I've been following fiber optics development through my private broker/investor and in night courses with a local university.

I'll be visiting in the Northeast in a little less than a month. I'll call you within a few days of this letter to set up a possible get-acquainted meeting.

Sincerely,

David C. Halpern

Enc: resume

COVER LETTER
IN RESPONSE TO AN AD

□

Advertisement

Personnel, Assistant Manager
Opportunity for Personnel Administrator with experience.
Employment, training, grievances. Assist in negotiations.
Degree in Personnel or Industrial Relations + minimum 2
years' experience. Eastern Pennsylvania manufacturer.
Send resumes to Box 17A.

Letter

May 12, 1992

Box 17A
New York Times
New York, NY 10036

Ladies and Gentlemen:

My four years of intensive personnel experience, plus my Industrial Relations degree from Cornell, qualify me for your job opening for an Assistant Personnel Manager.

I have just completed my military obligations, where I had full responsibilities for employment, training, and employee relations for civilian as well as military personnel. My Cornell education covered union-management relations in depth.

A personal interview would give both of us the opportunity to explore this further. I am willing to relocate anywhere and can visit your plant next Wednesday or Thursday, since I will be in the vicinity.

Sincerely,

Donald J. MacArthur

Enc: resume

Step 10. Alternative to a Resume

Some people have job targets where resumes are inappropriate. Among these are people who have been out of the work world for several years—a housewife, a sculptor, or people who took a year off to travel, who have been ill or incapacitated, or who are just beginning careers. This group also includes people who wish to change fields radically.

Here are two ways to handle these situations.

One is to have someone you know who is in touch with your employer target write a letter of recommendation for you. Better still, write the letter, then have your friend type it on his or her own business stationery, sign it, and send it.

The second way is to write a letter to your employer target, similar in form to the functional resume, and no longer than two pages. It should be based on your history, accomplishments, and problem-solving skills and how these relate to the job target you want. Your letter to your employer target should reflect the value your background can bring to the organization. Represent your creativity through your use of accomplishment-oriented paragraphs. List benefits you can bring, despite the fact that your immediate experience is not in the area of your job target. Good research into the employer's needs will help you focus on these benefits.

RESUME ALTERNATIVE
□

This letter comes from a woman who wants to enter the work force after many years at home. Because she has not held any full-time jobs, she emphasizes aspects of her background most closely related to her goal: a job in marketing.

Barbara H. Ashford
123 Douglas Street
Wichita, Kansas 67211
316-555-1122

February 19, 1992

Mr. Sheldon Sosna
Vice-President—Marketing
Household Cleanser Corp.
78 Washington Street
Wichita, Kansas 67208

Dear Mr. Sosna:

Our mutual friend, Burton Bell, suggested that I contact you concerning a position in your marketing department in which I could make a significant contribution. My marketing accomplishments include the following:

. . . As assistant to the fund-raising director for Community Chest, I divided the territory into districts based on census figures and estimated contributions by district with 92% accuracy. This resulted in considerable cost savings in subsequent campaigns.

. . . As part-time market research supervisor locally for a major household products company I determined the viability of introducing three new products.

. . . Supervised seven part-time researchers in house-to-house survey. Survey reports were vital to later marketing.

. . . In last three statewide elections, coordinated political party's vote analysis program in my district.

. . . Wrote sales promotion material for membership drive for United Cerebral Palsy chapter, resulting in largest number of new members since chapter was organized.

. . . Sold Avon products (part-time) for eight years. Always in top ten of region.

My formal training in marketing includes:
B.A.—University of Kansas—major in Economics.

Special courses—Wichita State College:
  "Marketing Research Methods"
  "The Computer as a Marketing Tool"
  "Advertising and Sales Promotion"
  "Marketing Consumer Products"
  "Accounting for Non-Accountants"

I am confident I can be a valuable addition to your marketing staff and would appreciate the opportunity to meet with you within the next few days. I'll call for an appointment.

Sincerely yours,

Barbara H. Ashford

RATE YOUR RESUME

Use this form to rate your resume or that of your friends, or to allow your friends to rate *your* resume. Grade the resume in each of the categories as excellent, average, or poor.

	Rating			Suggestions for Improvement
	Excellent	Average	Poor	
Does it stress accomplishments over skills and duties?				
Is the resume clear? Is it easy to get a picture of the writer's qualifications?				
Is irrelevant personal information left out?				
Does it avoid self-evaluation?				
Is the language clear and understandable?				
Does it emphasize benefits for a potential employer?				
Is it well-printed on good professional looking stock?				
Does the layout invite attention? Do strong points stand out?				
Is industry/product line of past employers clear?				
Do the sentences begin with action words?				
Does it sell the writer's problem-solving skills?				

15

---□---

CONTROLLING
THE INTERVIEW

The interview is the main event. It is the result of your many steps in self-discovery, targeting, research, and communication. Given what's been invested in it, the interview should be treated with concern, respect, and creativity. No matter how you have fared until now, the whole quest can be achieved in the interview.

Many assume that the interview is an employer-run show—they ask the questions, you answer them. Not true. The clear-thinking candidate can do a lot to influence the outcome of the interview. The interview is one of the most important opportunities to manage the job-search process.

As a serious career voyager, your prime assignment is to learn how to control each interview. Controlling the interview means keeping it moving in the directioon *you* want it to go.

INSIDE THE EMPLOYMENT INTERVIEW
□

A job interview is a meeting between two human beings to discover the extent of their mutual interest in working together. The employer goes into the interview wanting to hire you as much as you want a job offer. The interviewer wants to find out if you are the person to solve a particular problem. An interview exists because a resume, application form, or a phone call can't tell enough about a job or a candidate.

From the employer's point of view, an interview is a conversation in which the hiring authority tries to make an accurate prediction about your future performance in the company. It is usually a comparative process. First, against the standards or objectives of the job possibility, and secondly, against other candidates for the job. Clearly, having targeted the employer, your task is to show them how hiring you will create a big payoff for them. Once the employer is interested in you, the time will come when you will want to find out if the company and job is of interest to you. Create the employer's interest first and then do your own appraisal. (It is easy to turn down an offer when you get it.)

What the Employer Wants to Know About You

During interviews, the employer will usually attempt the following:

□ To verify the accuracy and completeness of your resume and application form and to resolve any gaps or apparent contradictions.

□ To quantify the information you gave. (For example, say you were a country club manager. How many members? What was the fee total? Were you responsible for recruiting new members? If so, how did you do? Did you manage a monthly budget of $50,000 or $150,000?)

□ To appraise your verbal skills. This includes your ability to sensibly and interestingly respond to questions with originality and sincere interest. Canned responses can lose you a job offer.

□ To probe your experience and accomplishments, and to evaluate their pertinence to the present job possibility.

□ To judge personality or social factors (interpersonal skills, etc.) that may be relevant.

□ To describe the position and note your response and interest.

□ To determine salary requirements.

PREPARING FOR THE INTERVIEW
□

The best interviews result in offers. The preparation for the meeting should start long before you appear in the employer's office. Many candidates do little to prepare for interviews. A large portion of this chapter is devoted to helping you maximize your impact in interviews. Solid advance preparation can give you a considerable advantage over other candidates for the job.

Interview Planning Form

Take a look at the Interview Planning Form on pages 200–201. We recommend you use a copy of this form for each interview you have. The form will help you organize in advance all the information you can possibly manage that might be relevant during your job interview. The various items on the form are explained below.

PART I: ABOUT THE EMPLOYER

Employer Name, Address, Time, and Date of Interview: Get the correct address. If there are multiple offices, the interview might be at an address other than the one with which you've been in touch. If the location of the building is unfamiliar, get explicit directions so you are not late.

Individual Giving the Interview.   Get the exact name and title of the person with whom you are meeting. Also, get the name and title of the person who will make the hiring decision.

Job Description.   Even if you feel familiar with the nature of the job, write down as detailed a description of it as possible. Don't be shy about calling the secretary or the person who is interviewing you to ask for additional information.

Salary Range.   Prior to your interview, accumulate as much information as you can about the salary range in this job-target area. If you know the range in advance, you will be in a better position to negotiate salary.

   You can get salary information by contacting officers of trade associations or people you know who are in the field. Another tack is to contact a placement counselor who deals in the field to see if he or she can give you an idea what the going rate might be at this firm or at comparable companies.

Products and Services.   You should know the major products and/or services that the employer produces or delivers to the public. You should also know the responsibilities of the department or section for which you are being interviewed.

Competition.   Know the relative position of the company within the industry. Are they among the larger or smaller firms? Are they growing or declining? The more you know about your potential employer's competition, the more you may be able to show yourself to be of value to them.

Public Image.   How does the company's public image compare with its industry image? Find out what people in the same business think of them.

History.   The higher the job level, the more you must know about the company's past, present, and future. At any level it's wise to know what major changes occurred in the recent past and what trends are apparent in the near future.

Day-to-day Problems.   Before your interview, try to find out the kind of day-to-day, month-to-month problems faced by the person who would hire you. Those problems could be budgets, turnover, sagging contributions, supply shortages, complaining customers, low productivity, overload or overwork, poor organization. You want to get this information in as specific terms as possible.

PART II: ABOUT YOURSELF

Use Part II of the Interview Planning Form to organize the data about yourself in a way that will aid you in communicating the maximum value you have to offer.

Review Your Resume.   Is all the information complete? Can you account for all the time since you started full-time employment? If there are gaps, have an explanation planned. If you are not sure of the dates of specific events, check.

Work Accomplishments.   In the interview you will be asked to provide information about your previous positions, education, and special training or skills. List at least one accomplishment from each experience that is slanted toward your present job target.

Private-Life Accomplishments.   Often, accomplishments in one's private life can contribute to one's aptness for a job in the commercial world. Write down personal accomplishments on this part of the form.

Possible Problem Areas.   Anticipate any areas in your past that might stand in the way of your getting the job offer. Review these points and prepare strong responses to questions you could be asked.

Questions to Ask the Interviewer.   There are two types of questions to prepare here.

Work-oriented questions will help your decide about the quality of the company, and where it is going. "Who are the firm's major competitors, and how are they doing?" "What is this company's strategy for being a leader in the field?" "What are the newest technologies most appropriate to the work you will be doing?"

The second type of question to prepare in advance is about specific elements of your prospective job. This category is not about vacation and benefits, but more professional matters such as:

- What are the job's day-to-day duties? (Do they meet with your concept of work pleasure?)
- What is the working style (participative, highly managed, tight, loose)?
- How much authority will you have over decisions?
- What is your growth potential one, two, and five years hence?
- To whom does your future boss report?
- What happened to the person who last held the job you want?
- What would be the best continuing education for you to consider if you were to have the job?

Note: Before the interview, prepare six to eight questions in advance on the form provided or on an index card you can take with you to the interview.

Use the following Interview Planning Form, or one like it for every interview you have. Fill in as much information as you can in advance, and obtain additional information during the interview. Review the form before and, if possible, during the interview. Review it carefully after each interview.

INTERVIEW PLANNING FORM

□

Prepare this form in advance of each interview you take.

Part I: About the Employer

Date & time of interview _____

Your job target _____

Interview is with _____

Secretary's name if you have it _____

Employer name _____

Division or department you are interviewing in _____

Address of interview (directions to get there, parking, etc.) _____

_____

_____

Phone _____

Descriptions of position applied for _____

_____

_____

_____

Salary range (if known) _____

Products & services of employer _____

_____

_____

Competition _____

_____

_____

Day-to-day problems of employer _____

_____

_____

_____

_____

Public image _____

_____

_____

_____

Brief history _____

_____

Other information about the employer _____

_____

_____

_____

Part II: About Yourself

Review of resume data complete? _____

Main past work accomplishments _____

_____

_____

_____

_____

Private-life accomplishments _____

_____

_____

_____

_____

Possible problem areas _____

_____

_____

_____

_____

_____

Questions to ask the interviewer _____

_____

_____

_____

_____

_____

Other information to prepare _____

_____

_____

_____

_____

THE INTERVIEW FORMAT
□

An interview is a structured conversation between the interviewer and you. It will usually, though by no means always, follow a logical format. Here is one typical format.

1. Introductory: warming up the space.
2. General: Description of the job.
3. Opening request: "Tell me about your recent work in this field."
4. Specific request: "Have you worked with multilingual teams?"
5. Verify: "How did your work with Kodak relate to your work with Polaroid?"
    [The interview will repeat sections 3, 4, and 5 as necessary with subjects.]
6. Tough questions: "How do you think you would handle this work without understanding French?"
7. Over to you: "Is there something you would like to know about us?"
8. Ending: "We will get back to you soon to let you know what we are thinking about the next steps."

Here's an important strategic point to consider: Even though it seems as though the interview is on one track, there is no reason that you need to follow the tour that is laid out. To control the interview, you will want to use every opening to ensure that you communicate the information that is essential to your presentation, and that you do this smoothly.

In general, the way to go about this is to use the power of questions to shift the flow of the conversation from the interviewer's control to yours. For example in step 4 above (a specific request) rather than merely answering say no, you might say "No, I haven't worked directly with multilingual teams; however, I have worked with many diverse cultures, and found it easy to communicate. Do you require multiple languages for your international staff?" If the answer is yes, follow with "I've always been a fast learner, and could probably polish up my French if it were needed. On the other hand, my experience in debt swaps across many countries is very strong. Would you like to hear more about it?"

In other words, shift the emphasis to your strongest qualities.

You can use open-ended questions to obtain as much information as possible from the interviewer. Most interviewers are happy to talk at length about the job when asked. Be a good listener as well as a good questioner. You need this information to help you evaluate the job and the company and to give you clues to what kinds of answers will impress the interviewer. You might ask: "What personal qualities would you say are most valuable to perform this job successfuly?"

Many interviewers maintain control of the interview by using lots of closed questions. These are questions that can be answered in one or two words. Closed questions, which tend to sound like a Ping-Pong match (with fast responses on both sides), generally keep the control of the interview firmly in the hands of the person asking the questions—which is usually the interviewer. The major disadvantage to the questioner is that he or she doesn't have much time to evaluate the answers given before it's time to ask the next question.

INTERVIEWER: You say you grew up in the hotel business?
    YOU: Yes.
INTERVIEWER: You have a degree in hotel management from Cornell?
    YOU: Yes.
INTERVIEWER: In your position with Saddle River Resorts were you responsible for catering the conventions?
    YOU: Yes.

When this line of questioning prevents you from expressing ideas you want to communicate, parry with the straight answer and then continue immediately:

YOU: Not only was I responsible for catering the conventions, I also ran the two restaurants. You know I studied at the Culinary Institute for one year after graduation. Originally we had much the same kind of restaurant problem you have here, but I reworked the menus and we soon turned a profit. Would you like me to tell you a little about it?

Probe questions are a form of cross-check or request for more specific information about an area already discussed. Here are some examples:

INTERVIEWER: You mentioned that your previous supervisor was quite difficult to work with. Could you tell me more about that?
INTERVIEWER: Why do you want to change fields after ten years in education?

INTERVIEWER: What exactly were your responsibilities as production manager?

Sometimes, probe questions are simply an effort on the interviewer's part to get further clarification. However, sometimes they are intended to uncover contradictions, inconsistencies, unfavorable attitudes, and so on. Be prepared for them by knowing what your weak points are and by thinking through your answers.

Probe questions are useful for you. Although it is important to be a good listener, the surest way to impress people with your seriousness is to ask intelligent, penetrating questions about the position and the company, such as:

YOU: Tell me more about the company's policy on promoting from within.

YOU: Why did you decide to give up the computer franchises after only one year?

YOU: Will the company back this new product with national advertising?

Twenty-one Questions

Listed below are twenty-one questions that come up in a variety of interviews. Not all are necessarily related to your own interview, since questions vary from one job to another.

Answer each relevant question in the space provided below it. You can write your answers in an abbreviated form because your verbal responses may be rather lengthy. The object is to list the key points you want to cover in your answer.

First, write in the appropriate space the name of the potential employer and a brief description of the job target for which you would be likely to be interviewed. Address your answers to this prospective interviewer—speak them aloud if you wish.

Your Job Target _____

Name of a prospective employer _____

_____

Abbreviated job description _____

_____

1. What was your most important accomplishment during your school years? _____

2. Which subjects did you like best and why? _____

3. What was your poorest subject in school, and why? _____

4. Why did you leave your last job? _____

5. Can you work under pressure? _____

6. What is your biggest weakness? _____

7. How long would you stay with us if this job were offered to you? __

8. What other positions are you considering? _____

9. What can you offer us that someone else cannot? _____

10. What did you like least about your last job? _____
_____
_____
_____

11. What position and salary do you expect to hold in five years? _____
_____
_____
_____

12. Why are you interested in working for us? _____
_____
_____
_____

13. How long do you think it would take you to produce tangible results in this job? _____
_____
_____
_____

14. What is your opinion of the company for whom you currently work or previously worked? _____
_____
_____
_____

15. What about the position under discussion interests you the least? What interests you the most? _____
_____
_____

16. Do you like to work individually or as part of a team? Why?
_____
_____
_____

17. Can you supervise people well? Give an example. _____
_____
_____
_____

18. What do you think your co-workers think of you? _____
_____
_____
_____

19. To date, what have been your most important career accomplishments?

_____

_____

_____

_____

20. What is the minimum salary you would accept? _____

_____

_____

21. And, most important of all: Why should I hire you? _____

_____

_____

Now look back over your answers to the twenty-one questions. Ask yourself each question out loud, and then answer it without reading your notes.

Use a tape recorder if you have one. Play your answers back and critique them. You could have another person critique them with you or fire the questions at you.

Three Tough Questions

Next, think of the three questions you would find most difficult to answer—the questions you hope the interviewer won't ask. List them below.

1. _____

_____

2. _____

_____

3. _____

_____

Take a deep breath and compose answers to the three questions you hoped wouldn't be asked. Speak them aloud again and again, until you have what sound like satisfactory answers. In order to remember the answers, list the key words for each in the space below.

1. _____

2. _____

3. _____

Interview Control Techniques

When answering interview questions, it is important to keep the following in mind:

- □ Watch for oral and nonverbal feedback from the interviewer. Do his or her eyes wander or fingers tap? Are there signs that interest is wandering? If so, shorten your answer or switch to another topic.
- □ Leave out superfluous detail, and stress all the benefits you can convey.
- □ If you don't know the answer to a technical or factual question, say so. Nobody knows everything.
- □ If the interviewer is someone who knows little about your particular skill or technical field, don't rub it in. Discuss the subject in a general and interesting manner.
- □ Don't agree when you don't agree. An honest difference of opinion is acceptable if it's expressed in a thoughtful, nonhostile way.
- □ Save some of your strongest self-selling points for the end of the interview.
- □ Take your time, think about your answers before giving them, and try to remain relaxed. And listen, listen, listen. The earlier you can get the interviewer to talk about the position, the company, or the department, the more you can sense what he or she is looking for and the more directed your answers can be.
- □ Refer to your own questions about the job and the company as you go along. Make sure to convey the impression that you too have to be sold.

THE ANATOMY OF AN INTERVIEW
□

Interviewing styles will vary greatly from employer to employer, and from person to person. Some managers and supervisors, as well as some personnel people, are very poor interviewers, even though they may be otherwise excellent at their jobs. Regardless of the personalities involved, as we indicated above, there are several main stages in an interview. Here are some more insights and strategies for three main stages.

Stage 1: The Opening

At the start of the interview, establish a cordial rapport with your interviewer. Shake hands, introduce yourself, and relax. Don't make small talk unless the interviewer seems to want to put you—and herself—at ease. If you have a moment to look around, note the surroundings and the office decor. Pay attention to any personal touches that will give you some idea of the interviewer as a human being, not an authority figure. Remark on any trophies, paintings, or other signs of the interviewer's interests. Don't overdo it, but if the interviewer is responsive, you can explore these interests for a few minutes.

The average interview will last anywhere from thirty minutes to an hour. In the opening minutes, the interviewer should tell you how much time is scheduled. If she neglects to do so, ask, "How much time do we have?" so you'll know how long you'll have to make the points you want to get across.

If the interviewer talks at the opening, listen attentively. If she waits for you to begin, do so and have a well-prepared lead ready that relates to your job target. For example: "I'm quite impressed with your marketing approach—building a family of products around an established toothpaste name. Where did the idea originate?" This kind of open-ended question forces the interviewer to answer.

Interviews that you have "created" within the hidden job market particularly require that the opening statement be your responsibility.

Stage 2: Information Exchange

After about one-third of the interview has elapsed, you should know both what the employer is seeking in the position and the day-to-day requirements of the job. In the second part of the interview, the interviewer will want to get information from you in the following areas:

EDUCATION, TRAINING, AND SKILLS

This will include degrees, grades, major subjects, specific skills, and other training related to the job target area. Keep in mind that schooling will be less important when you have been out of school more than five years.

WORK EXPERIENCE

If you've been in the work force for three or more years, this experience is more important than schooling, especially if you are applying for a position in the same field. Most commonly, the interviewer begins with open-ended questions, asking you to describe your experience. When answering, spend as little time as possible describing responsibilities and accomplishments in jobs that are over five years old. Of course, you should stress these jobs if they were significantly different from your most recent experience, or if they are important to your new job target.

During the interview you may refer to your resume or to written notes. Use this material for quick reminders.

When describing previous positions, emphasize problem-solving areas most related to the current needs of the prospective employer. As noted earlier, keep watch for nonverbal and oral signs of the employer's response to your remarks. If she shows signs of losing interest during your presentation, break up your remarks by asking her questions such as "How do you handle it here?" or "I think that what we did might be similar to the kind of approach you took in your scheduling—is that right?"

Your questions will be based, of course, on your pre-interview research.

PERSONALITY FACTORS DESIRED

These are never clearly spelled out; nor are they easy to determine through direct questioning. But if the interviewer has done her own preplanning, she will have five or six specific characteristics in mind that she will try to uncover. Below is a list of the most common personality factors that show up in job descriptions. They are in no particular order. Before your next interview, try to imagine which four or five might be most important for your specific job target.

Professional appearance	Motivation	Initiative
Self-confidence	Positive attitude	Creativity
Self-expression	Resourcefulness	Punctuality
Alertness	Stability	Aggressiveness
Maturity	Leadership	Neatness
Sense of humor	Growth potential	Attention to detail
	Team player	Versatility

Intelligence	Innovation	Easy, relaxed
Warmth	Perseverance	manners
Sensitivity to	Honesty/sincerity	Vitality
feedback	Naturalness	Dedication to work

Stage 3: End Game

By now you will have a good feel for the fit you may have with the job. Be sure you are comfortable with that fit. A mistake here is worse than buying a pair of running shoes that give you horrible blisters, because this bad fit could last for years and finally blister your spirit. There is no need to be caught up in getting the interviewer to like you. It's you who must be comfortable so that you can do your best for the company and for yourself.

This is the final quarter or so of the interview. At this time you should make an appraisal of how you have done so far. If no clues have been forthcoming, ask: "Does my experience seem to fit what you are looking for?" or "Is there any area of my experience that you'd like to know more about?" Listen closely to the answer. If the answer is noncommittal, push—it is appropriate to say something like "I think that my experience would be valuable to your organization. Do you agree?" Most applicants never ask this question, but they should. If you haven't asked this of your interviewer, now is the time to find out, not two weeks from now in a form-letter rejection. If you've made a good impression, such questions won't change the interviewer's mind.

If the interviewer expresses uncertainty that you are the best candidate, try tactfully to find out why. "Is there some particular area of my qualifications that you feel doesn't meet your requirement?" In a comfortable, nonconfrontational way, inquire about specific points that might keep you from getting the job. Suppose the interviewer says "The problem I see is your lack of familiarity with the new AXJII storage-retrieval technology." If you don't have an immediate comeback, say you'd like to think about the point she raised. Do think about it, and then get back to your interviewer with an answer in a follow-up letter or a telephone call. If you don't have requested skills, rather than feel embarrassed about it, shift to your positive qualities. For instance, say "No, I don't have that experience [or skill]; however I'm a fast learner and could probably pick this up with a bit of training."

YOUR QUESTIONS

Bring up the questions you have prepared about the job and company, as well as any questions that occurred to you during the interview. They show serious concern and a concrete understanding of the company's problems. Questions such as "Do you have five-year projections for this division?" or "Are you satisfied with the profit margins that you've developed in this product line?" are not too aggressive. The answers represent the kind of information that a serious candidate would want to know about a company.

CONCLUDING THE PERSONNEL INTERVIEW

If your interview was with the personnel department, as many will undoubtedly be, your objective is to try to get a commitment for an interview with the proper hiring authority. Ask "Do you think it would be possible to meet with Ms. Walters now, or this afternoon?" or "When is the earliest time I could meet with Mr. Barlow? I have several other job opportunities pending and before I make any decision, I'd like to explore this one more fully. Would it be possible to set up a meeting this week?"

UNSUCCESSFUL INTERVIEWS
□

If you and/or the interviewer have decided that you are not right for the position, that's not the end of the line. Having established a face-to-face relationship, there is still much that can be done. Ask the interviewer about positions in other organizations or about people you might contact in an extension of your job search. Get names and addresses and write them down.

Most important, try to get as much feedback as possible as to why your interview failed. This information should pertain to how you came across personally, areas in your resume that might be improved, etc.

Don't be embarrassed to ask. If the questions are put in the proper way and you communicate a genuine, nonhostile desire to learn, you may be surprised at the cooperation you receive.

SALARY NEGOTIATIONS
□

Because salary questions can be one of the touchiest points in an interview, the interviewer and the applicant will often avoid them as long as possible.

Before going to an interview you should know as much as possible about the general salary ranges in your field. This can be uncovered by some preliminary research with people in the field, trade associations, or perhaps employment agencies specializing in the field. When the interviewer asks, "What is the minimum salary you will accept?" do not name a specific figure. Say "I wasn't going for the minimum; what is the range you have in mind?" When a salary range is given, always verbalize the top of the range.

EMPLOYER: The salary range is $18,000 to $22,000 per year.
    YOU: $22,000 is in the ballpark.

If you are asked your present level of earnings, include your full compensation plan—including benefits, medical, bonuses, etc. Since most firms do not confirm present earnings, if you are somewhat general, the specifics will generally go undiscovered.

Another useful strategy is not to accept the offer at the time it is made, even though you are interested. Let the employer know you appreciate the offer, and that you need a little time to think about it. "Can I get back to you next week?" shifts the game from the employer thinking you need the job to wondering whether or not you will accept his offer. This also gives you time to decide if you are interested in the job for the right reasons—satisfaction and growth or pure survival. If you want to pursue the offer, it is perfectly all right to negotiate. Seldom will a firm withdraw an offer simply because you feel you're worth more than they want to pay. Instead, they will probably make a counteroffer. By being willing to negotiate, you demonstrate your value. If a company won't budge from their first salary offer, you might compromise with items like earlier-than-normal salary review, stock options, a bonus plan, and so on.

PRACTICE MAKES PERFECT

What you say influences what the interviewer says, and what the interviewer says influences what you say. A good interview can be a satisfying experience for both—the negotiation could affect both of your lives. Nevertheless, it is an experience that most individuals have only a dozen or so times in their lives—if that often. It is also an experience that, from the applicant's point of view, can be clouded by nervousness, worry, and anxiety.

The employer needs you as much as you need him. You aren't just an applicant for a job—you are a unique being, with a combination of skills, capabilities, and interests. Remember, you must not confuse the job description with yourself. The interview, even more than the finest resume, is the point where the human element takes over and where you can transmit your special qualifications and attributes directly and most convincingly to the prospective employer. It is your best chance to play down your shortcomings and to maximize your positive values in terms of your job context.

Given the normal job lifetime, you may never handle enough interviews to become really proficient at the art. So the best way to give a professional, relaxed interview is through practice. By doing so, you will learn how to transmit your unique and special value.

One form of practice is to go on interviews for positions you are really not interested in and ask for and get as much feedback as possible from the people who interview you. Another, even more productive way of obtaining useful feedback on how you can improve your interviewing techniques is through the use of the role-play interviews.

Role-play interviews are structured practice interviews involving you and a friend or family member or another job-seeker. The basic requirement is that you project yourself into the role and be as realistic as possible. In the role plays, you can act as both the applicant and the potential employer at different times to obtain greater insight into the interview process. You can use the twenty-one questions on pages 204–207. If possible, you should have an audience of one or two other people to critique your performance and give you suggestions about how to improve it.

Finally, have fun! The interview is neither a sentencing or the final judgment on your career worth. The interview is a discussion between equals. Allow yourself to know that you are as valuable and unique to the person you are talking to as they are to you. Enjoy the opportunity to find out, engage, challenge, and present your best.

16

---□---

CLOSING IN
ON THE DEAL

This is no time to stop. Assuming that you have done the work of targeting, research, and contacting and that you've ended up with several decent interviews, the temptation is to kick off the shoes, pop open a refreshing libation, and wait for the employers to take care of the next steps. You're right—that's wrong!

It is natural to ease back a little when you have pushed beyond a number of the more serious obstacles and have had some successful interviews. You put up your feet, relax and then . . . drift into the Sargasso Sea of waiting for the actual offers to come in. And then, day by day, the disappointment sets in. You learn one important thing about employer responsiveness—there isn't much. Even if there is serious interest and there are no other candidates, the average employer seems to take about six weeks from final interview to firm offer. Yes, there are many exceptions in both directions. Of course, in more cases than we would like to recount, the expected offer doesn't materialize.

If you are smart you will observe this cautionary principle: The overly awaited offer rarely arrives—act appropriately. Why does the offer not come? Budget changes, the other candidates, the one interviewer in the cycle that wasn't sold. Postponements, travel schedules, and all the rest of the litany of deferral and turndown are other major factors to contend with in the last stages of your career voyage. Therefore, sail on and keep all hands on deck until you have landed the job you want: offer in hand, offer accepted, and starting date set.

So we turn to perhaps the most important domain of all—follow-up strategies for closing the deal. We divide this section into two parts:

1. All the things you need to keep your eyes on in the job campaign, to keep the process going and gain more interviews.
2. Strategies for keeping pressure on the employers with whom you have interviewed to get them to make the best offers—to you!

First of all look at the Action Checkpoints below. Check any of them that are true for your campaign, circling the right word when a choice is given. (If you are just browsing at this point, come back when you have launched your job campaign.)

ACTION CHECKPOINTS
□

_____ I haven't thoroughly worked out my list of accomplishments and skills.

_____ I haven't mapped out a job plan yet.

_____ I've asked some people for information on my job target, and they haven't gotten back to me. I haven't gotten back to them either.

_____ I need to put in a little more time preparing additional resumes.

_____ I have skipped a number of exercises in this book.

_____ I have several pending phone calls to make to employer targets.

_____ I planned to send letters to a number of employer targets and I haven't done it yet.

_____ I sent out cover letters and resumes weeks ago. No response.

_____ I was going to get in touch with ——— and haven't done so.

_____ I have an interview scheduled and haven't found out much about the department or the company.

_____ I want to see what's happening at an employment agency, and haven't done so.

_____ Whatever happened to that interview with ———?

Additional statements _____

_____

_____

_____

If this list revealed a number of inactions, you need some follow-up. Take action! Do it now!

FOLLOW-UP TACTICS

□

The second part of follow-up is with employers with whom you have had interviews. The purpose of a good follow-up campaign is to accelerate response *and* to push for getting the job offer. Those are two quite separate objectives. If the response is absolutely negative, you want to find it out quickly and keep moving. On the other hand, the essence of follow-up strategy is to intervene at those moments when the decision-making process is in flux so that you can ensure a positive outcome. If the timing and strategy are right, you can even reverse turndowns. Here are some proven, practical follow-up strategies.

Urgency

Whether you are waiting anxiously or peacefully, too much waiting around is not productive in a job campaign. You must impart a sense of urgency to every step in this campaign, and you must communicate that to the prospective employer. Stay on follow-up timetables. If the employer says he will get back to you in a week, and ten days go by, call him.

Additional Information

Providing additional information is an adaptable follow-up device that can be used at any point in your job campaign after you have made your initial contact with your employer target. Any additional information should add new benefits to your approach and give you a fresh positive push. It is both a means of staying in touch and of giving the employer another reason to make you an offer.

Repeat and Recap the Benefit

If at first you don't convince, repeat and repeat again. That's why TV commercials bombard us with the same sales message over and over. Your personal commercial will not suffer from repetition. It will be remembered.

Therefore, if you don't hear from a prospective employer, follow up with a recap of the benefits you have to offer. Write or telephone to remind her of who you are and what your problem-solving capabilities are in relation to the company's opportunities.

Response to a Question or Problem

If something interesting has come up in an interview or a phone conversation, use this as a lead to a follow-up contact. The question or problem could be one concerning the position or the company, or one that relates to your qualifications. Sometimes, coming up with a practical solution to the question or problem will require that you do a little research. But now that you know how to do this, it's not that hard.

For example, in an interview for a position as executive chef for a large hotel, the hotel manager mentioned that they have a major problem with high staff turnover. You make a mental note. A week after your interview you send a follow-up letter in which you say:

> I've been thinking about your problem with high staff turnover. One approach I might suggest is giving incentive bonuses to people who have stayed for a certain duration. I know that this has been tried successfully with [a West Coast hotel chain], and it worked out quite well.

Going Beyond the Personnel Department

If you are rejected by personnel, acknowledge their decision and imply that it was your responsibility that they did not have all the information they needed. Don't even imply they could be wrong. However, be prepared for the fact that the higher-up you went to see may have made the decision himself, but had personnel send out the letter.

If possible, try to get in your appeal to high authorities before you have been officially notified of a rejection. This way you are not necessarily defying the system—just trying to be helpful.

Here is an example of an approach that works:

> Mr. Rachlin, this is Paul Mickle. I'm sorry to interrupt you—I realize you're busy, but I'm in your neighborhood now and felt it might be valuable for both

of us if you could see me for a few minutes. Several weeks ago I had an interview in response to an advertisement about an opening in your section as a contract negotiator. I've had three years solid experience in negotiations in both commercial and military projects for an organization like yours.

I've heard from personnel that I am being considered for the position, but I'm in a bit of a spot. There are two other situations that I'm now considering, and I'd like to know as quickly as possible about your opening, which I'd much prefer. Since you are the one who will make the final decision, I'd like to bring a copy of my resume over and meet with you for a few moments.

The New You

If the job is worth it, you can redo your resume and send it back to the employer as an "update," with a powerful follow-up letter. This is particularly easy to do if you are using a computerized resume preparation kit.

Third Party Follow-ups

One of the proven methods of getting you closer to a job offer is to have other people take positive action. Let's examine how they can help you:

A person who has referred you to an employer for an interview often has a relationship with the person at the organization to which you were referred. She can use this relationship to expedite action. If nothing is happening, she can find out why. If there is a problem, she can find out what it is.

For example, if the employer has narrowed the decision down to two or three candidates, and you are one of them, she could ask a question like "What are Harry's strong and weak points for the position?" She might be more likely to get a direct answer than you would. Armed with this information from the "agent," you might just happen to drop by or call, providing some additional information to build up your case.

Both before and after your interview, there are some other things that a third party can do to help you. For example, he or she can:

□ Find out from the potential employer before the interview what particular aspects of the job are the most important and what the salary range is.
□ Make sure that the resume or interview is directed to the highest-ranking decision maker, and follow-up to see that it gets there.

□ Find out the immediate reaction to the resume or interview and help you decide how to reinforce positives and overcome negatives.

□ Imply a sense of urgency in making a decision, suggesting to the prospective employer that you may be considering other situations.

REFERENCES

One of the most effective follow-up techniques is when one of your references is a person of some standing in the field—prior employer, a college professor, a politician, etc.

Whether it is after your interview or before, you may feel in need of some positive encouragement in your campaign. At this point, ask your reference to call the individual who is responsible for the hiring decision and to put in some good words for you: "Mr. Jones has asked me to be a referral for him, and I am calling to let you know about his work with me . . ."

Turning Turndowns Around

When you have been turned down flat in your approach to a job target, don't take no for an answer!

If there is a job you truly want, and somewhere along the line you've reached a point of frustration, don't just pick up your marbles and leave. It is possible that an extra effort may turn the situation around; if not, at least you may obtain valuable additional feedback that will help you in the future. The first step in this approach is to find out why you weren't hired. Only a very small percentage of job-seekers even consider this tactic. Upon receiving a negative response, the prevailing tendency is to withdraw—feeling hurt, rejected, depressed, and/or discouraged.

An adage among top salespeople is The sale doesn't begin until the prospect says no! This means that the salesperson must meet and overcome the real objections or restrictions that the potential buyer has.

The same goes for you. As a job-seeker (a salesperson selling yourself), you must face the objections that an employer might have. This is a natural part of the process of getting what you want. There are many kinds of turndowns or objections that you will encounter in your job campaign. Let's recap some that we have discussed before:

□ In response to a letter or resume you sent, a form letter says sorry—no openings or nothing for you just now.

- A turndown on a request for an interview—either by phone, mail, or in person.
- A letter or telephone call after a personnel-level interview informing you that "despite your fine qualifications, we are unable to make an offer at this time."
- No response at all.

The reason you have been given may not be the real reason at all. The innocuous bureaucratic expression "Unfortunately, at the present time we have no openings which fit your qualifications" may cover any number of possible reasons. These include:

- We've got too many applicants for this job already—we really don't want to consider any more people.
- We've narrowed our search down to three other candidates and will probably decide on one of them.
- You don't have the specific experience we seek.
- We didn't see what we were looking for on your resume.
- We've decided to hold off on filling this position for a few months.
- You don't have the degree of education we seek.

There are also several dozen possible reasons, including the fact that the employer might actually have someone in mind who they think is better for the position.

The rejection may come in response to your sending in a resume to someone you've never met or talked with. In this case it will be more difficult to find the real reason than if you had actual contact with someone. Of course, this is one of the reasons we are against the indiscriminate mailing out of resumes—it gives you no personal connection.

It is different when your rejection comes from someone you have met or with whom you have spoken. Here, good telephone technique can get you the kind of feedback you need to overcome the turndown or at least to tell you something that will improve your next interview. For example:

Mr. Mack, this is Harold Steinman. We met two weeks ago regarding the position in your collections department. I got your letter today saying that you had decided that I wasn't the best one for the job. I want to thank you for the fast response, and the courtesy of the personal letter.

> I'm calling to ask you a favor. Could you possibly give me a bit more information about where my qualifications fell short? I have no issue with your decision, but it would be valuable for me in my future interviews to know where my strong and weak points are.

Sit back and listen and take notes, encouraging Mr. Mack to go on, particularly with the areas in which he feels you could have done better or been better qualified. Encourage negative responses—this is the best and also the most difficult feedback to solicit. Don't try to defend and answer these negatives—not now.

If Mr. Mack is reluctant to give you the information you need, you can ask specific questions such as "Could you tell me if you felt that my daily interest accumulation method had any applicability to your business?" or more personal ones such as "Are there any specific ways in which I could improve my interviewing presentation?"

It's not easy to get this information because most people don't want to have to criticize. Therefore, your skill in handling this difficult situation can make an impression; it says: Here's a person who is really interested in this job and can take criticism and learn.

After you have gotten all the feedback you think you can get (or stand), there is one more important thing to ask the person who has turned you down for a job:

> Thank you very much, Mr. Mack, you don't know how much I appreciate this. I'll think about what you told me. There's just one other thing I'd like to ask you. Could you suggest the names of any other concerns like yourselves, where I might make a contact for a similar type of position—or is there a particular agency you use that serves this field well? Or would there be someone in another part of your company who might have something appropriate for me?

Parlaying contacts is very important. It can be done at every stage of job seeking—once you've made contact, during an interview, or during follow-up. Probing for additional leads, whether within the same organization or out of it, is a proven way to get personal referrals to other job situations. This is a fine time to do it.

17

---□---

YOU ARE NOT ALONE

All the Help You Can Get

The search for a brighter future is often uncomfortable, and we can feel stranded and out of touch. We have the idea that something so personal has to be accomplished privately and courageously.

As a career voyager up against a challenging assignment, you need the partnership of others—practical day-to-day support as well as morale-building relationships. A prime source of this help, of course, comes from those nearest you: your spouse, friends, and relatives. Where possible, professional counselors, mentors, and co-voyagers who are more than casually involved and knowledgeable about the tasks ahead can also provide valuable assistance. Working with others will greatly increase the speed and effectiveness of your job search.

❖ **Rule of the road:** *Share the game with others.*

When you have identified a personal support system, you can start out by letting each supporter read this chapter. After they have read it, discuss frankly the specific actions that they might be willing to take to help make your job search more productive.

EMOTIONAL SUPPORT

□

It is not unusual to feel insecure and vulnerable when undertaking a job search or career change. If you are unemployed, financial insecurity can increase the distress. It is hard to avoid the feeling that somehow you are outside the system, looking in. Furthermore, the prospect of rejections—an inevitable part of every job campaign—can lower the spirits of the bravest, unless you see these rejections for what they are—steps towards success in obtaining targeted career objectives.

Memo to Personal Support System

Here's how you can help the job-seeker get over some of the emotional unease which can interfere with a job campaign:

□ Support the premise that a time of job change is a time of possibility, one that can reinvent the future in satisfying and exciting ways. Keep the quest away from the survival level.

□ Take a practical interest in the various steps in the process. Pay attention to successful completion of each step, small or large, and reward it with approval. The job campaign can be seen as a series of small wins, not as an excruciating process with the only finish line being an accepted offer. Reinforce the idea that rejections and disappointments are a natural part of the process.

□ Encourage the job-seeker to be involved in things other than the job search: physical and mental exercise, relaxation, family time, learning. It is not a good idea to immerse oneself totally in the employment campaign.

FINANCIAL SUPPORT

□

The time of job change is generally a period to conserve resources, to budget and plan carefully, and to gather all the support you can to keep you solvent. Although in some cases taking the next thing that comes along is unavoidable, the consequences of having to leap too soon into a new job can be devastating. All too frequently you then accept underemployment, lower pay (the employer who knows you are a bit desperate has greater negotiating power), and the lack of choice of opportunity that comes with jumping too quickly. In order to give yourself the maximum chance to secure the kind of job you deserve, you may have to obtain financial help from family and friends. As embarrassing as it might be to borrow, it is definitely something you should consider if this is what is required to do the right kind of work search. The payoff of taking the right actions to secure the right position to build your future is important enough to ask appropriately for help.

Before you call Uncle Charlie, Mom, or your in-laws, however, do your homework. Work out a budget, calculating how long you can comfortably (not luxuriously) get along on the assets you have, including unemployment insurance, if any. Then make a realistic appraisal of how long it will take you to conduct your job campaign. Add a month or two to give yourself the advantage of turning down any job offers that are wrong for you. If you then find you have to borrow money from friends or family, put the job plan and budget figures before them. Let them see what you are asking for is an investment with a real payoff—higher long-term earning power, and a brighter future.

Memo to Support System

- [ ] If you are a wife, husband, or someone sharing financial responsibilities, do what you can to help ensure that there is a practical, realistic budget in writing, and help your partner keep to it.
- [ ] If money has to be borrowed from friends or family, do what you can to help make these requests in as persuasive and business-like a way as possible.
- [ ] Limit discussion of money and economy to times when it is essential. It doesn't help to dwell on the subject endlessly. Try to deflect as much of the pressure as possible.
- [ ] If you are working, are there any conveniences to your job (an available telephone, office supplies, etc.) that you can ethically put at the disposal of your friend or spouse?

BRAINSTORMING

□

Throughout this book we have asked you to look at the idea of work and jobs in a new way. We invited you to explore new avenues of personal pleasure and accomplishment that might lead to work.

The free associating you did in relation to job families and job targets could represent important changes in career direction. In mastering the hidden job market you used imaginative ways to do job research and created new ways to get interviews and accomplish powerful follow-up. Originality is required in much of the job-finding and job-creating process. Ideas grow faster and better when worked out with others. Use one or two members of your support sytem for once-a-week informal rap sessions during which you discuss ideas about your career campaign and job plan.

Memo to Support System

□ Don't wait to be asked to participate in the creative parts of your friend's job campaign. Look at some of the earlier chapters of this book. See where you can contribute new ideas or challenge old assumptions.
□ Think of other people who can help, and put your friend in touch with them.
□ Don't be shy about suggesting your own ideas about areas of work or research from which your friend might profit. See if you can extend your thinking and your friend's beyond the rigid confines of the conventional.

NETWORKS

□

You should know by now that we set great store on all the contacts, friends, associates, networks, etc., that might be useful in your career voyage. Use your personal support networks wherever you can. The best source of new contacts is the existing network.

Memo to Personal Support System

□ List as many people as you can think of who might know (or have ideas about) work areas or contacts that your friend should know about. (You might want to read chapter 12, "The Hidden Job Market.")

- Call friends, relatives, and business acquaintances to see what leads they might have which could be valuable. Drop all fears about these calls. People *do* want to help. Many of the leads will not produce a big result, some will. It only takes two or three really good ones to open exactly the right doors.

FEEDBACK AND ROLE PLAYING

An important aspect of every good job campaign is to find out how you are coming across to others. Get the most accurate feedback possible, before and after you approach prospective employers. With the right preliminary feedback, you will know how to make the best impression when it counts—in the actual job campaign.

Use your personal support system as much as you can to critique your resume, your phone presentation, and your interview style, all before actually putting them to work for you in your campaign. Role-play with different members of your support team until you are satisfied that you have perfected your communication skills.

You may have to work to get good feedback, because people are usually shy about giving personal criticism. State at the beginning that you are looking for real feedback on those things which can be improved. When people correct you, don't explain or argue—simply acknowledge the information. Then ask for more, using leading questions: "How can I change the way I dress to be most appropriate to this group?" or "Thanks for being so open; what else should I do?"

If specific items of your job campaign seem to be giving you problems, discuss these openly with one or two friends or family members. Invite constructive criticism.

Memo to Personal Support System

- Feedback and critique are requested to provide as much helpful information as possible and to improve performance in presentation and activity in the job search.
- Be as direct as you can in suggesting alternative behaviors. The art of good criticism is to learn to say "I think this would be better" rather than "You're wrong."

FAMILY COUNSELING

□

Consider the impact on a marriage or important personal relationship of a significant career or job change. Financial worries or changed life-style habits may provoke a natural kind of resentment or tendency to blame or criticize. This is natural. However, just as insecurity can be catching, so can adventure. The success of any job campaign hinges frequently on the quality of the personal support from the family.

Changes in family income can raise questions that should be dealt with immediately and openly explored for answers. For example, if one spouse's income was the mainstay of the family, will the other consider working harder or take a second job so that the job-seeker can pursue a brilliant job campaign? If you are a two-career family, what happens if you find your ideal in another part of the country? How will you decide relocation questions? Try to get this clear up front.

In working out the answers to these questions and in dealing with other pressures that job changes bring about, you might find that the relationship gets strained. If you reach the point where you can't resolve the emotional load we suggest you consider family counseling. Don't be embarrassed by the idea—hundreds of thousands of couples do it. If necessary write to Family Service Association of America, 44 East 23 Street, New York, NY 10010. This well-recognized nonprofit organization, which has been operating for over sixty years, will put you in touch with an accredited family-counseling agency near you to help you work out the serious family strains that can be brought on by career stress.

Memo to Personal Support System

□   Do not be surprised if resentment, regret, and disappointment spring up when the person closest to you has external problems that challenge the status quo. Don't be surprised if your partner seems to take her problems out on you. Count to ten before responding to a negative. Look for the strongest assets, and bring them into day-to-day conversations. Don't be surprised if your partner doesn't want to talk about it. Draw out the partner's worries, fears, and perplexities.

- ☐ Be a coach. Set up times to work together, and times to be apart. Acknowledge positively when a major effort has been accomplished.
- ☐ Help organize the job search. Be familiar with the ideas of this book, help in exercises and in planning to take action. Help hold to schedules and if possible provide help in role playing, research, phone calls, etc.
- ☐ Remember, every career voyage needs a good first mate.

18

---□---

NO, NO, NO, NO,... YES!

Perhaps you have now plowed through this book with a notebook at the ready, organizing your own customized action plan. Perhaps you've put many of the strategies to use and have already accelerated your progress to powerful job offers.

If your job search is already well launched, if you have had interviews and negotiated offers, we salute you and wish you well in the next stages of your adventure in the career world.

If you have arrived at this point ready to engage in action, break open the directories, make the calls, write the letters, print the resume, and so forth. This marks not the end, but the beginning of your own self-motivated, intelligent career search. We invite you to continue to use the book as a set of maps—selecting your own routes through and around obstacles. We caution you not simply to follow our tactics as if there is only one *right* way to conduct your career voyage. The most important strategy for you now is smart action, exercised promptly with energy and intention. Experiment with other ideas and do what works best for you.

Decades of experience have convinced us that a thoughtful approach to career development works. We also know that strategy without action is simply game playing, and that action without strategy is blundering. It's up to you to pull together your own combination of thinking and action.

It's important to reprise our main theme: Our work spans the greatest part of our lives. It is the vehicle for our self-expression, consumes most of our time, is the source of many of our most meaningful relationships, and fundamentally determines the quality of our lives.

Remember that there is no scarcity of jobs. Break out of old boxes and move into realms of opportunity and problem-solving.

In this decade and beyond, learning is key. It is important for you to learn how to learn and to keep on learning. Participate in volunteer activities, keep your health and energy high, economize but don't be traumatized by the idea of unemployment if you don't have a job right now. Embrace career entrepreneurship and the idea that you create your future. You are not a victim; you are an initiator. The job market responds to your requests.

Career voyager, fare thee well.

NOTES

NOTES

□

NOTES

□

NOTES

◻

NOTES

□

NOTES

NOTES

□

NOTES

□

NOTES

NOTES

□